THE

DANCING

PLAGUE

THE STRANGE, TRUE STORY OF
AN EXTRAORDINARY ILLNESS

JOHN WALLER

Published by Sourcebooks, Inc.
P.O. Box 4410, Naperville, Illinois 60567-4410
(630) 961-3900
Fax: (630) 961-2168
www.sourcebooks.com

Originally published in the UK in 2008 by Icon Books, Ltd.

Library of Congress Cataloging-in-Publication Data

Waller, John
  [A Time to dance, a time to die]
  The dancing plague : the strange, true story of an extraordinary illness / John Waller.
      p. cm.
  Originally published: A time to dance, a time to die. Thriplow [England]: Icon Books, 2008.
  Includes bibliographical references and index.
    1. Chorea, Epidemic—France—Strasbourg—History—16th century.
2. Strasbourg (France)—Social conditions—16th century. 3. Strasbourg (France)—Biography. I. Title.
  RC389.W35 2009
  362.196'83009443954—dc22
                            2009007866

Printed and bound in the United States of America
POD 10 9 8 7 6 5 4 3 2

To my grandparents

CONTENTS

ACKNOWLEDGMENTS

In making the arguments that follow I am deeply indebted to the prior scholarship of a number of historians, including Justus F.C. Hecker, Alfred Martin, George Rosen, Francis Rapp, and, above all, H.C. Erik Midelfort. A number of colleagues and friends have been very generous in translating key texts or helping me to improve my language skills: Anita Bunk, Harrison Kalbach, Laurel Ponist, Roland Demars, Laurent Dubois, and Nicole Weber. For fruitful discussions or editorial comment I am grateful to Michael Waller, Richard Graham-Yooll, Abigail Waller, Adrian Horne, and Katherine Dubois, as well as to Laurel Ponist, Daniel Dougherty, Ben Smith, Sean Dyde, Mark Largent, Robert Root-Bernstein, and Michael Salzberg. Several teachers are responsible for introducing me to the late medieval world and inspiring me to write about it: Thomas Eason, Jeffrey Grenfell-Hill, Maurice Keen, and Michael Mahoney. Susan Waller and Adrian Horne were invaluable assistants while in Strasbourg. And I would also like to say a special thank you to Gabrielle Feyler, Conservateur of the Musée de Saverne, for her exceptional hospitality. F. Kuchly of the Societé d'Histoire et d'Archeologie de Saverne et Environs, Special Collections of Michigan State University Libraries, the Albertina in Vienna, and the Dombauarchiv of Köln, Matz und Schenk, have all kindly permitted the reproduction of images. In addition, I am grateful to my students at the University of Melbourne and Michigan State University for fruitful discussions about the meaning of the dancing plagues. A travel grant from the Sesquicentennial Fund of MSU's History Department helped fund my research in Strasbourg.

Madnesses of the past are not petrified
entities that can be plucked unchanged from
their niches and placed under our modern
microscopes. They appear, perhaps, more like
jellyfish that collapse and dry up when they
are removed from the ambient sea water.
—H.C. Erik Midelfort,
Madness in Sixteenth-Century Germany

To every thing there is a season, and a time
to every purpose under the heaven:
A time to be born, and a time to die;
a time to plant, and a time to pluck
up that which is planted;
A time to kill, and a time to heal; a time
to break down, and a time to build up;
A time to weep, and a time to laugh; a time
to mourn, and a time to dance...
—Chapter 3, *Ecclesiastes*

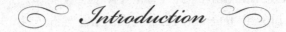

THE DANCING PLAGUE

JULY 14, 1518

S omewhere amid the narrow lanes, the congested wharves, the stables, workshops, forges, and fairs of the medieval city of Strasbourg, Frau Troffea stepped outside and began to dance. So far as we can tell no music was playing and she showed no signs of joy as her skirts flew up around her rapidly moving legs. To the consternation of her husband, she went on dancing throughout the day. And as the shadows lengthened and the sun set behind the city's half-timbered houses, it became clear that Frau Troffea simply could not stop. Only after many hours of crazed motion did she collapse from exhaustion. Bathed in sweat and with muscles twitching, she finally sank into a brief restorative sleep. Then, a few hours later, she resumed her solitary jig. Through much of the following day she went on, fatigue rendering her movements increasingly violent and erratic. Once again, exhaustion prevailed and a weary sleep took hold.[1]

On the third day Frau Troffea rose to bruised and bloody feet and returned to her dance. By now, one contemporary recorded, dozens of onlookers had gathered, drawn by the sheer oddness of this remorseless spectacle. Tradesmen, artisans, porters, hawkers, cripples, and ragged beggars jostled with pilgrims, priests, monks and nuns, and proud members of the patriciate: nobles set apart by their jewels, demeanor, and sumptuous robes, and the wealthier burghers sporting fur-trimmed gowns and expansive turbans of folded silk.[2] They watched as Frau Troffea's dance went on deep into the third day, her shoes now soaked with blood, sweat trickling down her careworn face. Speculations flew among the onlookers. We are told that some blamed restless spirits, demons that had infiltrated and commandeered her soul. Perhaps through sin, they said, she had weakened her ability to resist the Devil's powers. But the crowd soon decided that this affliction had been sent from Heaven rather than Hell. Accordingly, after several days of violent exertion, Frau Troffea was bundled onto a wagon and transported to a shrine that lay a day's ride away, high up in the Vosges Mountains. But if the authorities imagined that divine rage had now been quelled, they were quickly disabused.

Within days, more than thirty people had taken to the streets, seized by the same urgent need to dance,

Half bird's-eye view of Strasbourg by Franz Hogenberg,
contained in Georg Braun and Hogenberg's *Civitates
Orbis Terrarum* published in 1572.

hop, and leap into the air. In houses, halls, and public
spaces, as fear paralyzed the city and the members of
Strasbourg's privy council despaired, they danced with
mindless intensity. They went on day and night, in
clogs, leather boots, or barefoot, their limbs aching
with fatigue, their heels bleeding copiously, probably
some with sinews torn to the bone. By early August
1518, the epidemic had begun to spread at an alarming
rate. The numbers of afflicted rose each passing day
so that soon at least a hundred citizens were dancing
with crazed abandon. Within a month, according to

one chronicle, as many as four hundred people had experienced the madness. And sometime in late July, just a week or more after Frau Troffea had started to dance, the epidemic had taken on a cruel new face. A manuscript chronicle held in the city's archives tells of what happened next:

> There's been a strange epidemic lately
> Going amongst the folk,
> So that many in their madness
> Began dancing,
> Which they kept up day and night,
> Without interruption,
> Until they fell unconscious.
> Many have died of it.[3]

Exactly how many fell dead we cannot know, though one chronicle suggests that (at least for a time) fifteen were dying each day as they danced in the punishing summer heat, seldom pausing to eat, drink, or rest. Only in late August or early September 1518 did the epidemic finally subside, leaving many people bereaved and thousands more, in the city and beyond, fearful and bewildered. For over a month this terrible sickness had thrown into turmoil one of the largest cities of that sprawling collection of provinces and principalities known as the Holy Roman Empire.

This book tells the story of the dancing plague and seeks to explain why hundreds of people lapsed into a state of frantic delirium lasting days or even weeks. In doing so, it draws on a wide range of historical records, the analyses of several modern historians and insights from the disciplines of anthropology, psychology, and neuroscience. Even amid the other horrors of the early modern age, the events of this dreadful summer lived long in people's minds. Strasbourg's crazed dancers had acted out one of the oddest dramas in recorded history, and so bizarre had it been that details were carefully recorded, in Latin and High German, by scores of different writers. Local merchants, officials, preachers, even the architect who redesigned the city's defensive fortifications left behind descriptions of the dancing mania. A few of these chronicles were compiled during the period of the epidemic itself. Others were pieced together, fifty or more years later, from caches of manuscripts stored by the civil authorities and from conversations with those who'd been in their youth in the early sixteenth century. There are also municipal orders relating to the epidemic issued by city leaders, as well as sermons and the descriptions of leading physicians. Having survived in the city archives for generations, the originals of some of these accounts were destroyed by high explosives during the Franco-Prussian War of 1870. Fortunately, much of the material had already been copied or transcribed by local historians and antiquarians. And from these diverse manuscripts we can now create a fairly clear picture of the events that led to this terrifying plague.[4]

We owe the most detailed accounts of the epidemic to an irascible but brilliant alchemist and physician named Theophrastus von Hohenheim, better known as Paracelsus. He arrived in Strasbourg in November 1526 having spent much of the winter on the road, spurned by the elite physicians of other imperial towns as a medical heretic and suspected sorcerer. After passing through the Black Forest and across the Alsatian plain, he entered a city whose inhabitants were still trying to make sense of the bizarre horrors that had unfolded before them during the summer of 1518. Fiery preachers meanwhile reminded congregations of the dancing plague sent down by a wrathful Heaven to punish vile sinners. Paracelsus was fascinated. Self-proclaimed adept of the preternatural realm, whose mystical treatises were crowded with nymphs, demons, goblins, sprites, and elves, he was determined to work out the meaning of this strangest of afflictions.

The explanation for the dancing mania offered by Paracelsus bore his characteristic blend of skepticism, mysticism, and misogyny. He blamed Frau Troffea for her own wretched state. Noisy, idle, and vindictive, she'd started to dance to humiliate her pitiable spouse.

Only later did an irresistible urge take possession of her mind and body. In a mystical treatise of 1532, *Diseases That Rob Men of Their Reason*, Paracelsus dubbed her disease "*chorea lasciva*" and its victims "choreomaniacs." Those whose thoughts are "free, lewd, and impertinent, full of lasciviousness and without fear or respect" are liable, he said, to develop a "voluptuous urge to dance." The "whores and scoundrels" who succumb, Paracelsus went on, need to have their deviant imaginations tamed by being locked in "a dark, unpleasant place" and fasted on "water and bread." Alternatively, he added, they might fashion images of themselves in wax or resin, transfer their thoughts and images to the model, and then cast it into a fire.[5]

In three books written during the decade following his arrival in Strasbourg, Paracelsus returned to the subject of the dancing madness. It's just about possible, however, that he had heard of this mysterious affliction prior to arriving there. His father's modest library high in the Swiss Alps contained a work by Johannes Trithemius, a German abbot and mystic, in which he described a terrible outbreak of dancing mania that spread across the Low Countries, Germany, and northeastern France in 1374.[6] In fact, as many as seven bouts of uncontrollable dancing had occurred in various parts of western Europe prior to 1518.

The first is said to have taken place in a Saxon

town called Kölbigk in about 1017 when several people danced riotously in a graveyard until an affronted priest cursed them to dance for an entire year.[7] Unfortunately, it's not clear if the Kölbigk legend is a parable based on a true event, or parable alone. No less ambiguous is a Welsh chronicle entry for the year 1188. Its author, Giraldus Cambrensis, told of an annual religious ceremony that took place at St. Almedha's church in South Wales during which dozens of people danced and sang around a churchyard until they "fell to the ground," whereupon they began to enact "whatever work they had unlawfully done on feast days"—some pretended to be mending shoes, others to be drawing thread, and another to be operating a loom. They worked "as in a trance," while tunelessly singing popular songs. Although they were clearly engaged in a ritual, the strange behavior of these Welsh Sabbath-breakers has tended to be ascribed to the same cause as that which triggered the dancing mania of 1518.

German chronicles of around the same time speak of another apparent case of involuntary dancing. In the imperial town of Erfurt, during the year 1247, one hundred or more children are supposed to have danced and hopped out of the town's gates. Having reached a neighboring settlement, they collapsed, sleeping by its walls and along the streets. The children were later found by their distraught and bemused parents;

by then some of them were already dead and others were afflicted with tremors and fatigue for the rest of their lives. Some scholars argue that this story refers to a dancing plague. While the claim is unprovable, the detail about the survivors' later symptoms does ring true. And it was only shortly after the Erfurt incident, in the year 1278, that about two hundred people in Maastricht are said to have danced irreverently on a bridge over the River Moselle until, as a divine punishment, the structure collapsed and they perished in the turbulent waters below. This too has been interpreted as a case of compulsive dancing.

Far exceeding all these outbreaks in scale was the late fourteenth-century epidemic mentioned by the monastic record of Abbot Trithemius and several other chroniclers. Beginning in the Rhineland in the summer of 1374, probably among pilgrims from the Empire's northern provinces,[8] it would eventually extend all the way from Aachen and Ghent in the north to Metz and Strasbourg in the south.[9] For several months, small bands of wild dancers wandered from place to place, spreading the affliction to local people as if by contagion. Chroniclers tell of thousands of men and women dancing while screeching with pain, leaping into the air, running madly from place to place and calling on the mercy of God and the saints. Perhaps the oddest detail of the 1374 epidemic is the claim that if sheets were not tied tightly around the dancers' waists, "they cried out, like lunatics, that they were dying." The dancers were assumed to be possessed by demons; some sufferers even roared out the name of a devil they called "Friskes." And while most appear to have recovered bodily control within ten days or so, many relapsed one or more times. In disorderly bands those who had only temporarily recovered their reason traveled to holy sites, losing themselves to trance and wild dancing on reaching their destinations. In one case, hundreds of those in a briefly lucid state converged on a lonely, derelict chapel not far from the town of Trier. There they "built huts with leaves and branches from the nearby forest" and then, "possessed by demons and greatly tormented by them," they resumed their dances. The epidemic subsided by the end of the year, though it may have struck again in northeastern France in 1375 and the imperial city of Augsburg in 1381. From Liège and Trier to Utrecht and Cologne, priests performed rituals of exorcism, they screamed ancient incantations down the throats of the afflicted, and they immersed others up to their chins in blessed water.

Of two far smaller dancing epidemics we also have records. The first took place in Zurich's Water Church, so called for the bubbling spring water that pooled before its altar. The minutes taken at a meeting of local notables record that in 1418 several crazed women danced in the church, unable to stop, as a crowd of onlookers gathered around them. Another small group of mad dancers is mentioned in the "miracle book" of the pilgrimage shrine of Eberhardsklausen, near the town of Trier, in an entry relating to 1463. In addition we know of several isolated cases during the fifteenth and sixteenth centuries, from Switzerland and the Holy Roman Empire, of choreomania gripping a single individual or an entire family.

The Strasbourg dancing epidemic begun by Frau Troffea was the second largest of Europe's dancing plagues. But as it occurred after the invention of the printing press and in a city with at least the beginnings of a formal bureaucracy, it's far better documented and by a richer variety of sources than any of its predecessors. Indeed, of all the outbreaks of dancing mania, this is the only one that can be reconstructed in detail. It also occurred at a critical moment in European history, when the Holy Roman Empire was teetering on the edge of savage religious wars and peasant rebellion. But if this account concentrates on the events of 1518, the earlier outbreaks will provide useful insights into the enigma of Strasbourg's dancing epidemic.

The explanations for the dancing mania offered by Paracelsus and his contemporaries have not aged well. Nor have some more recent hypotheses. Several modern authors have sought a chemical or biological origin for these dancing epidemics, and the chief contender has been ergot, a mold that flourishes on the stalks of damp rye.[10] Compounds produced by ergot can induce delusions, twitching, and violent jerking. Millers in Alsace seem to have been aware of the risk, for the ends of the wooden pipes through which flour poured into waiting sacks bore horribly distorted faces, now believed to be reminders of the hallucinations that could ensue if the flour had been contaminated with ergot.[11] These potent chemicals do not, however, allow for sustained dancing. Convulsions and delusions, yes; but not rhythmic movements lasting for days. And the agreement of chroniclers, physicians, and clergymen is emphatic: the people danced. They may have hopped and leaped about too. There were no doubt also spasms and jerky movements, but witnesses in 1518, as in 1374, used the Germanic word *tanz*, meaning, unmistakably, "to dance." There are two additional reasons to reject the ergotism hypothesis. First, it is simply not feasible for hundreds of people to have reacted in the same bizarre way to ergot poisoning. Second, while ergot can lead to delusions and spasmodic motion, it much more often causes restricted blood supply to the extremities, which in turn produces an awful burning sensation, gangrene, and, often, an excruciating death. Crucially, there are no reports of what was called "St. Anthony's Fire" from Strasbourg in 1518.

Other authors have explained the dancing plague as a form of hysteria, a physical expression of psychological distress.[12] This is a more plausible hypothesis but in itself it provides no reason for why the afflicted danced rather than, say, wept, shouted, fought, fasted, shook, or prayed. This book argues that the epidemic of 1518 did indeed prey on people suffering from the most acute anguish and fear. It was a hysterical reaction. But it's one that could only have occurred in a culture steeped in a particular kind of supernaturalism. The people of Strasbourg danced in their misery due to an unquestioning belief in the wrath of God and His holy saints: it was a pathological expression of desperation and pious fear.

So to understand how Frau Troffea's solitary dance came to engulf hundreds of people, we need to look at the vicissitudes of daily life in Strasbourg, at the traumas that belie Renaissance Europe's reputation as a golden age of fine art and even finer feelings. For this was a world of terrifying uncertainty in which poor harvests triggered famine, devastating scourges such as plague, smallpox, and the "English sweat" arrived suddenly to kill old and young, rich and poor, and remote communities regularly found themselves at the mercy of bloodthirsty bandits or foreign troops. This was the world, for many suffused with pain and dread, that inspired the nightmare canvasses of Hieronymus Bosch and the haunting image of "Christ as the Man of Sorrows" by fellow German Albrecht Dürer. And it was a world so glutted with misery that nearly all ranks of society drank and danced whenever the opportunity arose, with the intensity of those in flight from an intolerable reality.

At the same time we need to enter into the minds of a people who were hooked on a mystical form of piety. The inhabitants of the Empire in the early 1500s imagined their world to be the embodiment of cosmic conflicts between good and evil, God and the Devil. Church doctrine infused almost every activity with supernatural meaning. Several times a week, if not every day, people attended religious services rich in magical ritual, their nostrils filled with incense smoke and the air charged with Latin incantations. Observance of the Church calendar also set the rhythm of daily life, while saints' days marked the different phases of the year. Artisans even timed such routine tasks as the dying of cloth according to how long it took to mutter a Hail Mary or a paternoster.[13] And, amid the humdrum preoccupation of staying alive during the late medieval age, the period's poor hung on keenly to the prospect of eternal bliss in the next life and did what they could to expiate their sins in ritual bouts of penance and prayer. It was in this fervently supernaturalist context that Frau Troffea, and then hundreds of her fellow citizens, succumbed to the dancing plague. As such, the story of the dancing mania takes us into a largely vanished world of arcane ritual, beliefs, practices, and fears. It explores a staunchly religious culture in which people took for granted that Satan and his servants stalked the Earth and that God and the saints hurled down arrows of sickness and death.

And yet this account of the crazed dancers of 1518 does more than tell of one of the most singular episodes in human history. It is also an exploration into the still relatively uncharted terrain of the human brain. In modern Western societies epidemics of dancing are virtually unimaginable. But the events of 1518 open a window onto some of the most extraordinary potentials of the human unconscious. Indeed, few episodes of mass hysteria come closer than the dancing plagues to defining the outer limits of what our minds can impel us to do in conditions of extreme distress. At the same time they draw our attention to the diverse ways in which psychic stress is articulated today. While the social and intellectual contexts have changed, the structures of our minds have not. So this book concludes by examining subsequent manifestations of the kinds of impulse that gave rise to the dancing manias of medieval and Renaissance Europe, including the writhing and blaspheming of "demonically possessed" nuns, soldiers of the First World War rendered mute through fear, and men and women from all ages paralyzed after traumatic

15

psychological events. All these psychic phenomena remind us of the ineffable strangeness of the human brain. But none more so than the deadly dance that began in Strasbourg in the summer of 1518.

We begin the story a quarter of a century before Frau Troffea was seized by a compulsion to dance. Reflecting on the traumas and the unbridled supernaturalism of these years allows us to comprehend why so many people, for whom tragedy and uncertainty were nothing new, spectacularly fell apart. Even in a period accustomed to sudden reversals of fortune, the decades preceding Frau Troffea's dance were exceptional in their harshness. Famine, sickness, and terrible cold blighted and ended thousands of lives in Strasbourg and its environs. At the same time, a succession of disastrous events, from the onset of syphilis to the remorseless conquests of the Ottoman Turk, convinced many that God had turned His fury upon the people of Alsace. Just as alarming, many more nursed the dreadful apprehension that most of their monks, nuns, and priests were far too idle and corrupt to be able to restore God's grace. From the last decade of the fifteenth century, the humble of Alsace showed an unprecedented restlessness, a new level of aggression, hostility, and fear. Empty bellies, gaunt faces, crippling debts, a profound distrust of landlords and clerics, and imaginations vibrant with terrible visions of ghosts, demons, devils, and vengeful saints sapped the confidence of the poor in their ability to weather life's storms.

This is a story of how a city's people lost hope.

PRELUDE:
COUNTDOWN
TO CRISIS

Chapter One

SIGNS OF THE TIMES

The portents for the new century did not look good. Many said it would be the last before Armageddon. In 1492, the year in which Columbus made landfall in the Caribbean and the Spanish monarchs expelled the Jews from their domains, a huge, triangular meteorite appeared over the horizon. Its luminous tail, streaking diagonally across the sky, was observed by a young boy near the town of Ensisheim, not far upstream from Strasbourg. He watched it, seconds later, thud into a nearby field. Alerted by the boy, a crowd of villagers rushed to the scene. Peering into a scorched crater, farmers, artisans, and field hands debated its significance.[14]

To the people of late medieval Europe things on Earth rarely happened by chance. Nearly every event had its origins in the supernatural. So when trying to find meaning for the unexpected, savant and serf alike looked up to where they imagined Heaven to be: beyond the last of the crystalline spheres in which the planets were said to lie. Others looked to the stars and planets themselves. Unlucky alignments of planetary bodies were said to unleash floods, famines, and plagues, determine the fates of empires and the course of individual lives. Many believed that God had created for everything on Earth an exact counterpart in the heavens; some even said there were as many fish in the sea as stars in the sky. And it was this symmetry between the earthly and the starry realms that allowed sages to prognosticate by working out future configurations of planets and constellations. Nearly every royal court had an astrologer whose study of stellar motions informed the pursuit of war, statecraft, and diplomacy. "By looking up I see downward," summed up Tycho Brahe, Danish nobleman and astronomer.[15]

Yet comets, meteorites, and asteroids implied a more direct, if coded, communication from God. And so, in the nearby city of Nuremberg, worried chroniclers speculated as to what horrors and natural disasters the Ensisheim meteor portended. Did it foretell the death of a king, a barbarian invasion, a wave of pestilence, or bloody peasant revolt? Meanwhile, the talented young lawyer Sebastian Brant, born in Strasbourg but studying in Basel, was convinced that this was a divine message with a clear purpose: God was telling His people to halt their wretched sinning.

Anonymous, *The Meteor of Ensisheim*, broadsheet
with text by Sebastian Brant. Published in 1492.

In December, Sebastian Brant wrote a broadsheet
with a woodcut image of the Ensisheim meteor crashing
into fields before the moat that encircled the town.
Beneath lay Latin and German rhymes telling of God's
righteous anger at his wayward people. Christendom
was steeped in vice, said Brant. Miserable sinners all,
His children had forgotten both Christ's sacrifice and
the awful flames of Hell. As a result, God had allowed
the Muslim armies of the Ottoman Turk to destroy
the ancient Christian empire of Byzantium. For Brant
the Turkish advance could only be interpreted as a
punishment for collective sin. For how could anyone
feel that God still loved humankind when He permitted
the infidel to gnaw at the flanks of Christendom? And,
while the Turks geared up for fresh onslaughts, the
Empire's princes feuded recklessly with their new
Emperor, Maximilian I, and the French king threatened to invade his lands.[16]

Brant begged the Emperor to restore faith and reason. Maximilian, partial to Brant's analysis of worldly affairs, traveled to Ensisheim and had the giant fallen stone placed in a local church as a reminder of God's wrath over the rank sinfulness of the times. He also reiterated his determination to mount and lead a Crusade against the Turk. But as the Sultan's disciplined and battle-hardened soldiers conquered the eastern Mediterranean, others went to apocalyptic extremes. For some, the awesome power of the

Albrecht Dürer's portrait of Sebastian Brant.
Silver point drawing of 1521.

Ottomans brought to mind the prophecies of the Book of Revelation. In paintings and woodcuts they appeared with sharp chins and narrowed, ferocious eyes, bent on Christian bloodshed. It seemed that Satan had been "loosed out of his prison." "Gog and Magog" had come bringing slaughter and ruin. The Beast waited in the wings.[17]

Brant anticipated further disasters and humiliations for Christendom, but did not yet foresee the end of the world. By their wickedness humans had forfeited God's love and they'd have to mend their ways to restore it. Having completed his law degree, Brant now emerged as a leading humanist, dedicated to restoring purity to religion and Latin discourse. And, as he studied the morals of the clergy upon whose piety so many depended, he recoiled in disgust.

Back in Brant's birthplace of Strasbourg, another humanist and scholar, Geiler von Kaysersberg, had spent the last decade upbraiding monks, nuns, and priests for their vulgarity and worldliness. Geiler's admirers dubbed him "the Trumpet of Strasbourg Cathedral" and came hundreds of miles to hear his oratory. The cathedral of Notre Dame, in which Geiler preached, soared magnificently over the city, its rose-colored spire, façade, and rose window intricate as lacework and replete with hundreds of statues of saints, sinners, and devils. In the quiet coolness of the cathedral's interior, sunlight streaming through towering stained glass windows dappled the floor and columns with color. But if this was a place of great beauty, its resident canons were not always holy. And so, from a gorgeously carved stone pulpit, Geiler rebuked the clergy for setting the laity such a pitiful example. He did so with unfailing courage. His father had been killed while trying to protect villagers from a rampaging bear.[18] Geiler showed the same brand of fearlessness in taking on the idle, whoring, and rich-living clergy of the diocese, some of them scowling in the cathedral's shadows as he reproached them for endangering the people's souls. Not that he was always stern. Toward his congregation Geiler could be tender in the extreme. In fact, he had given up hearing confessions because he couldn't bring himself to impose stiff penances on those who had committed serious sins.

As Brant worried about the Ensisheim meteor in 1492, Geiler addressed a synod of the Strasbourg church on the issue of reform. Before a gathering of 600 clergymen, ranging from the highest-born canon to the humblest monk, he poured verbal vitriol. Monks and nuns were accused of fornicating and then murdering their bastard children; five children's corpses, he said, had been found buried in one local cloister.[19] Other monks and priests shamelessly took concubines. And nearly all had far greater appetites for meat, drink, and sleep than for prayer or pastoral duties. Geiler reminded the clergy of their responsibility toward the laity and that hatred for the Church grew daily. Now, at last, Albrecht of Bavaria, Bishop of Strasbourg, gave him the go-ahead to undertake a tour of religious houses and remedy their abuses.[20]

Most of the clergy left the 1492 synod chastened but determined to resist. In most monasteries and nunneries, the asceticism of medieval founders had been long ago set aside. Gone were the beds of straw, the bland fare, the exacting regimes of song and prayer, and the abrasive, louse-infested hair shirts which, in constantly itching the skin and tearing open boils from infected pores, were meant to remind wearers of Christ's agony on the cross. Many of the clergy, especially the canons and nuns, were the younger sons and daughters of nobles or wealthy burghers. They weren't willing to forgo the rich tastes and styles they had acquired in growing up. And so canons and monks wore coiffured hair, daggers strapped to their belts, and fashionable slippers; while nuns who were meant to don habits of unfinished and undyed wool and to spend their days in silence or prayer, were to be seen visiting taverns wearing jewels, belts sparkling with gold, and caps with ostrich feathers streaming behind. Rumors also spread far of them breaking their most intimate vows. A Dominican nun had recently been caught copulating with a hired workman. The abbess responded by locking the nunnery doors and banning males under fifty years of age from entering. This only excited gossip. After all, why would one need to imprison the sincerely chaste?

Unfazed by the hostility of the clergy, in late 1492 Geiler set out on his tour of inspection. Within the city walls and beyond them, he found several monasteries and nunneries in which monks and nuns lived exemplary lives. Already several Dominican houses had restored the pious indignities of old. But in most monasteries he discovered sweet breads, prime cuts of meat, and the finest vintages of wine in the darkness of underground larders and cellars. Most abbots, with plenty to hide, refused him admittance. And the monks of one monastery hinted darkly at murder when he tried to find evidence of bastards and concubines. Forced to abandon his mission, Geiler reflected that the bishop minded little: he preferred the income from levying fines against his errant monks to the ideal of clerical purity.

Geiler's campaign had enjoyed ardent support among the laity of Strasbourg. Many of them deeply resented clerical vice. The fact that the clergy were so often indolent and corrupt mattered to them because without honest clergy, their souls might not be purified by the sacraments. It mattered because if their souls ascended impure into the afterlife, they could expect to spend hundreds of years in Purgatory, the dismal antechamber to Heaven. And it mattered because souls uncleansed of sin might even be consigned to the everlasting torment of Hell. Thus, many pious citizens, both rich and poor, despised the clergy while fearing for their souls.[21]

Yet the tensions between Church and laity were as much political as spiritual. Until the mid-1200s the bishop of Strasbourg had ruled the city. Since then power had passed into the hands of an elite consisting of wealthy merchants and urban nobles who resented any efforts made by the bishop's palace to reclaim its old influence in civic affairs. The laity of Strasbourg owed its ascendancy to the city's geographical location. Lying alongside the mighty Rhine River, close to bridges and pontoons built by medieval engineers, Strasbourg commanded one of the Empire's principle waterways. It also lay astride several ancient trading routes linking by road, from west to east, France with Poland and Bohemia, and, from south to north, the Mediterranean with Europe's colder northern provinces. As a result, the city had become a wealthy commercial center, with tradesmen arriving daily from all parts of Europe. Merchants from Verona and Venice driving cart-loads of oils, spices, silk, and rice, even figs and raisins from the Ottoman Empire, reached Strasbourg having negotiated treacherous Alpine passes. From upstream, in Switzerland, there arrived consignments of coal, wood, logs, furs, skins, and leather in square-prowed, flat-bottomed boats. Nuremberg to the east sent the forged instruments of war: swords, daggers, stirrups, horse bits, and harquebuses. There were even carts laden with wool from the lush, lowland valleys of far-off England; as well as woven fabrics from Bruges, Brussels, and Ypres; silks from Paris; ribbons from Rheims; gold from Lombardy; hemp, sugar, and pepper from Antwerp; and from the Baltic and North Sea, kegs of salted cod and smoked herring. And in slim craft with jutting prows, propelled by long poles at the stern, local traders brought barrels of wine from the foothills of the Vosges Mountains for export to France, the Empire, even the court of Henry VIII. Its coffers filled by customs dues, the city resisted the worldly ambitions of the Church.[22]

In recent years the hatred of the clergy among merchants, traders, and artisans had reached new levels. For despite living lives of opulent ease, most canons, monks, and nuns paid hardly any of the taxes that oppressed the citizenry. This inspired contempt across social divides. Still less forgivable was their refusal to donate more than a token amount to help defray the huge costs of defending the city from attack. In 1475, with a threat of foreign invasion hanging over the city, the authorities had implored the clergy to assist in meeting the expense. Monasteries and chapters had refused with haughty disdain. Meanwhile, the secular elites, determined to restrict the political authority of the Church, did what they could to further blacken the reputation of the clergy.

The humble looked upon the Church's wealth with profound distaste as severe hunger took hold in late 1492.[23] This was the third year in a row that crops had failed due to freezing winters and torrential rain. Peasants who had had to consume every sack of wheat, barley, or rye now had to buy seed from lords and monasteries to sow for next year. In times like these they spoke with wistful relish, at the well, tavern, and mill, of a fabled land they called *Schlaraffia* in which food grew without the need for toil and fried pigeons flew straight into one's mouth. In private, and when tongues had been loosened by ale, some wondered if the sublime poverty of Christ was compatible with the worldly splendor of the Church. Others talked of a past golden age in which the rights of the poor had been respected and the priesthood cared lovingly for its flock.

There were no landlords in the peasant utopia of *Schlaraffia*, for the poor of the region knew that the rapacity of lords, monasteries, and chapters had deepened their plight. Agricultural prices had been falling for decades and, in order to shore up their incomes, many landlords had turned free peasants into bound serfs. Virtually everywhere they had imposed harsh new taxes, and if a peasant or farmer failed to make his annual tithe payment to the monastery, convent, or parish church, he was often excommunicated, condemned to live with the expectation of everlasting damnation. The victims of lords and clergy especially lamented the attacks on their ancient privileges. Across most of the Empire, peasants were now forbidden from grazing pigs on common pasture, from fishing in local pools and streams, and from entering the forests to gather timber for building and fuel, to hunt game, even to pick acorns or berries. Along the Rhine River in 1492, as hunger took hold, tensions rose.[24]

Word now spread of a proscribed book, covertly published by imperial printers, called *The Reformation of Sigismund*. It told of a simple priest who had come to the Empire to lead the poor against their oppressors. Its author lambasted priests for, among numerous other moral crimes, the sin of simony. Too many priests, he said, drew incomes from more than one parish and then paid half-educated lackeys a pittance to mumble through divine services in their absence. *The Reformation of Sigismund* thrilled thousands of Alsatian farmers and urban artisans with its talk of the holy slaughter of parasitic clergymen and greedy merchants.[25]

In Strasbourg itself, such eschatologies delighted a growing number of men who felt roughly treated by the city's elite. The poorest denizens, hawkers, porters, beggars, street entertainers, and farmers with small holdings in the suburbs, struggled for every mouthful of bread and swig of wine. But the gravest threat to peace and order came from the hundreds of apprentices, journeymen, and day laborers who toiled in workshops and kilns but were prevented by the city oligarchy from ever achieving the wealth and security of their masters. For these citizens, hard-working but out-of-pocket, decades of grueling labor brought few rewards.[26]

The dismal harvest gathered in late summer 1492 ensured that the lower ranks of society entered the new year suffering badly. Food reserves were quickly exhausted. Famine gripped the lowland plains and high-country of Alsace. And some freethinkers talked with a new conviction of a divine right to resist oppression. In early 1493 adventurous and angry young men, recruited among the fields, gardens, and vineyards around Strasbourg, plotted bloody revenge. The deadlines for the payments of rents and taxes were looming and many of these men, unable to pay up, faced the imminent prospect of homelessness and excommunication. They called their movement a *Bundschuh* in reference to the symbolic working man's boot that they planned to tie to a pole and hold aloft before their army. In March the conspirators gathered on a desolate hill where they swore an oath of secrecy. Just a few days later one of them reneged on his fellow rebels. They were swiftly rounded up. Most were hanged or beheaded. Yet while it was a strategic failure, the attempted *Bundschuh* of 1493 marked a new escalation in rural violence.[27]

In Strasbourg the magistrates were disturbed by copious signs of divine anger and civil unrest, so they set about overhauling the city's morals. They passed regulations restricting prostitutes to certain areas and prohibiting them from soliciting after nightfall. And so they couldn't be mistaken for godly women, prostitutes were barred from wearing fur or jewels. The privy council tackled gambling next, confining the players of cards and dice to the gambling den.[28]

But the pursuit of pleasure, an ecstatic, immoderate counterpoint to the hardships and uncertainties of daily life, went on. The local humanist, Jacques Wimpheling, railed against those who marked saints' days by rolling barrels of beer into the cathedral's chapels, dispensing it to the impious and prodding them out of their stupors when they collapsed, so that they could drink yet more. The high point of revelry was always the Lenten carnival. For several days before Lent, peasants and artisans who had spent what little they had on brightly colored stockings, impressive buckles, even lace shirts, indulged in days of hedonism. They danced around bonfires, watched raucous plays, drank freely, gorged themselves on roasted meat and dressed as popes, bishops, Turks, fools, devils, and beasts. In a spirit of carefree topsyturvydom, peasants were crowned as Kings or Abbots of Misrule and merchants and lords sometimes came disguised as serfs. Lewdness and gluttony prevailed, while beer, exuberance, and resurfacing resentments frequently spilled over into raw violence. Revelers fought with fists, sticks, and rocks, and they tortured the defenseless: Jews, dogs, cats, and fowl.[29]

The rest of the year offered more secretive or sedate forms of escape. Weddings, funerals, baptisms, and the induction of new priests entailed drinking, music, and dancing. Even monasteries and convents, to Geiler's disgust, hosted dances. And amid the sleazy humidity of the city's bathhouses, patrons of both sexes stripped to share baths, food, drink, and, for the amorous, discreetly curtained beds. The moralists fumed, but such entertainments were analgesics for those with few consolations and weighed down with dread and bitter memories. During moments of intimate intensity or days of drunken abandon, the cares of life briefly lifted. Intoxication gave a welcome release; insensate excesses for increasingly painful times.

Not that everyone indulged. In 1493, Sebastian Brant lent his weight to the crusade against vice by publishing his *Ship of Fools*, an unsparing satirical attack on the weak, hedonistic, and impious. Brant imagined a ship laden with fools and manned by fools on a journey toward a fool's paradise. There were 112 species of fool in his taxonomy, each of whom was mocked in woodcut and verse. Priests and monks came in for plenty of crowd-pleasing abuse. Brant damned monks as "incompetent monkeys" who entered monasteries just "to eat their fill." Written in German and produced in large quantities from the printing presses of Basel, *Ship of Fools* quickly became a bestseller. But Brant had a serious point to make: most humans, including clergymen, were going to burn in Hell for their folly.[30]

Divine judgment couldn't always wait. The grain harvests in 1494 were an improvement, relieving some of the agonies of the previous three years. But a novel and terrible sign of God's displeasure was soon to descend: syphilis would badly shake the confidence of Christendom.

It was carried to Strasbourg by mercenary pike men returning from the wars in Italy where they had come into contact with Spanish troops and the prostitutes who laundered their clothes and provided more intimate comforts. In early 1495, the executive head of the city, called the *Ammeister*, spoke of a "bad pox"— something new and awful.[31] Victims complained first of agonizing pain in their joints, which made sleep all but impossible. Soon after, the genitals, legs, face, and flanks became rancid with blisters, pustules, and ulcers. Geiler, from his pulpit, spoke of "mouths covered with pustules, the same in their private parts, arms, and legs and their entire bodies." And as the eruptions turned from red to black, flesh began to fall away. "It ate away the nose and half the face," recalled one; pustules and ulcers "gnawed away as far as the marrow." All shrank from the wretched sufferers, their skin and weeping wounds exciting horror and revulsion. Even lepers, pariahs of the age, refused contact with them, for their "putrefaction stank and [it was] a most awful filth."[32]

The citizens argued doggedly over the origins of what came to be called the "French Disease."[33] Lorenz Fries, a local physician, put it down to a conjunction of Jupiter, Mars, the Sun, and Mercury in the eighth house of the heavens. But most agreed with the humanist Wimpheling: syphilis was a carnal scourge. Beginning with blistered penises and vulvas, it obviously arose from venery. Syphilis was the *flagellum Dei*, God's whip, a stark warning about the sinfulness of adultery and fornication. In full accord, Brant issued a broadsheet depicting the Christ child, cradled by his mother, hurling down shafts of disease upon a group of sinners, their skin riddled with foul sores, one of them already prostrate and dying.[34] In sending this new affliction, God appeared to speak plainly. And in the weeks that followed the first appearance of excrescences on the

From the title page of Sebastian Brant's
1496 pamphlet on syphilis.

legs and faces of the Strasbourgeois, public processions
were held to beg for divine mercy, the air filled with
incense and the murmur of plaintive prayers.

Meanwhile, from a still unappeased God there
continued to pour forth cryptic messages. In 1495
Brant wrote another broadsheet about conjoined twins,
baby boys fused at the forehead, born in a small village
on the Rhine south of Strasbourg. Shortly after, he
issued another, this one accompanied by an Albrecht
Dürer engraving showing the "Sow of Landser," a
bizarrely misshapen pig with two extra legs in the rear
and another pair projecting from its back. For Brant
this was yet another coded exhortation for Christians
to wage war on the Ottoman Turk, a duty made all

the more pressing by the Turkish navy having recently sunk dozens of Venetian galleys and captured several Mediterranean islands.[35]

With each successive portent, Brant's readers were becoming ever more horrified. Then the evil signs came to a halt. For four years mild winters followed by temperate summers brought healthy harvests of wine and grain. Wheat prices fell to half of what they had been just a few years before and even Brant failed to see alarming portents in the skies, cribs, or barns of Alsace. The relative plenty of these years quenched some of the rage that had sparked the failed revolt of 1493.

Yet life had not returned to a benign normality. In the preceding years, a sharply discordant note had entered the rhythm of daily existence. Many among the lowest, or third, estate were by now convinced that monks, nuns, and lords had broken the sacred ties that were said once to have bound master and man together in mutual affection. Lords and clergy, unwilling to give up their luxuries in those arduous times, had oppressed the poor with a new and often savage contempt. Amid the poorer, filthier, and diseased quarters of Strasbourg, signs of disquiet persisted. Wealthy masters incited bitterness among their poorer brethren, apprentices, and journeymen. The well-heeled, rich-living members of the clergy still inspired disgust among the many who feared for their souls. The waves of mass suffering had calmed and thoughts of rebellion subsided, but beneath the surface there churned a maelstrom of popular discontent.

This was the disturbed world in which Frau Troffea was coming of age.

Chapter Two

PLAGUES AND PRIESTS

P lague followed famine. After four years of respite, the first year of the new century brought a meager harvest and empty bellies. Moving back to his native city of Strasbourg to become a legal advisor to the magistracy, Sebastian Brant could see burgeoning ranks of orphans and beggars. A year later, after a somewhat better harvest, ripples of panic spread across the city as news broke that bubonic plague had struck Mulhouse, twenty miles to the south. God was angry again.[36]

Hieronymus Brunschwig, surgeon and author of a book on the plague, instructed its victims to offer up prayers to St. Sebastian, St. Roche, and to the Virgin.[37] From his pulpit, Geiler scorned the magistrates for their lack of concern for the famished, sick, and dying poor of the city.[38] He spoke of the mothers who had recently lost sons and daughters to hunger and disease.

And with a tenderness rare among his peers and that spoke directly to the experiences of his congregation, he begged mothers not to "weigh down" their children's souls with their tears.[39]

Fatal maladies were a constant feature of life in this cramped Renaissance city. Piles of excrement from pigs, fowl, dogs, and horses collected in streets and courtyards. In alleys, beneath bridges, and between buildings the city folk squatted to defecate, their stools and foul odors lingering and attracting swarms of flies. Upper story latrines in the homes of the rich likewise spattered walls and cobbles with feces. Filth was ubiquitous. The slaked lime, used by tanners to strip hair and fat from their animal hides, polluted and discolored the water flowing through the city, as did blood from the pigs, boars, cows, and sheep having their throats slit by butchers in the abattoir on the river bank just south of the cathedral. Records show that hundreds of sheep were slaughtered there every day, their fluids and entrails washed into the river. High-pitched cries and squeals and the rank smells of scared and dying beasts floated in the air, while the water used for drinking and washing carried poisons and the germs of deadly disease.[40]

In the midst of syphilis and other forms of sickness, conflict within and beyond the city swelled once more. Somewhere along the Upper Rhine, probably in a monastic library well-stocked with works of macabre theology, an elderly fanatic composed an apocalyptic call to arms. It was called *The Book of a Hundred Chapters*. Although never published, this book crystallized the resentments of an age heading for upheaval. It spoke of a king who would ride "on a white horse" out of the Black Forest with "a bow in his hand" to lead a crusading army of the third estate against its oppressors. The king's humble followers would "drink blood for wine" as they ushered in a new golden age, restoring the equality of the Garden of Eden and the empire's primeval past. Obsessed with rich-living, wine-swilling, whoring monks and priests, the author called for them to be burned alive or sent as slaves to the Ottoman Turk. Each day 2,300 clerics would be massacred until all were dead or enslaved. Usurers and merchants were to be next.[41]

On the other side of the Rhine from Strasbourg, a young man called Joss Fritz, bound as a serf to a local abbey, sensed that these were ideal times for another *Bundschuh* revolt. We can assume that Fritz resented his bondage to the clergy and that he had been on the receiving end of their aggressive tactics as landlords. A man of enormous ability and charisma, he began plotting to purify the Church and to restore the rights of the common folk.

As grain prices spiked again, the agents of abbots and canons carelessly made Fritz's task easier. Having stored their grains given as tithe payments in commodious granaries until they could fetch a better price, they now sent word to local merchants who arrived with empty carts and purses of gold. Monastic records show that on some days eighty carts, creaking under the weight of tithe grains, were sent to nearby fairs.[42] This at a time when peasant farmers were once more having to beg and borrow to buy seeds for sowing the next year's harvest. Harnessing a rising tide of bitterness, Joss Fritz promised to flush out greedy monks, priests, and lords, firing up his recruits with an ideology of "divine justice," the peasant's holy right to restore God-given freedoms. His *Bundschuhers* felt that they were doing the Lord's work.

Preparations for the revolt were steeped in secrecy. Initiates had to recite five paternosters and five Ave Marias on their knees, and learn a virulently anticlerical password: "God greet you, fellow. How fares the world?" with the reply, "We cannot rid ourselves of the plague of priests."[43] More than one thousand peasants were ready to follow the *Bundschuh* banner, their martial resolve stiffened by several mercenaries. But then one of Fritz's mercenaries saw a safer way of turning a profit and informed the authorities. The ringleaders were mostly rounded up. Several were swiftly dispatched in a

An engraving of Joss Fritz by the German
artist Albrecht Dürer (1471–1528).

nearby palace courtyard, while Bishop Albrecht ordered
a full-scale manhunt along the east side of the Rhine.
Fritz himself managed to escape, probably fleeing into
the ancient heart of the Black Forest.

Another *Bundschuh* had been stamped out. Yet
at the start of 1503 the authorities in Alsace still had
much to fear. Wheat prices remained high, if not crip-
plingly so, and early indications were not favorable for
next year's harvest. In his fortified palace in the town
of Saverne, Bishop Albrecht fretted about the veiled

warnings once more being issued by Heaven. He decided to address a letter to the hundreds of priests in a diocese that stretched from the Black Forest in the east to the Vosges Mountains in the west. For some time, the bishop warned, "the sign of the holy cross" had been appearing "on the clothing of many men outside our territories." Now the same phenomenon had "appeared within the bounds of our diocese." Some of the evils portended by these strange apparitions were already in evidence. "We see that the Heavens have been closed," the bishop wrote, "rain has not fallen to relieve the dryness. The earth cannot bring forth fruit." Albrecht drew the typical conclusion of an age that saw God as the author of all natural disasters and the Earth as a timeless battleground between His and Satan's forces. The parched, cracked ground and the fields of desiccated crops spoke of more chastisements to come: "Danger is imminent," he wrote, "on account of our sins." Atonement was therefore imperative.[44]

We don't know if the bishop's flock heeded his warnings. For all the dignity of his title and noble birth, Albrecht's power was limited by his own deeply ingrained moral stains. Clerics were unlikely to feel compelled to put away their concubines or live abstemious lives when their bishop surrounded himself with overindulged courtiers and had fathered several bastard children.[45]

Yet even an exemplary bishop would have failed to curtail the sharp financial practices of the clergy. These days they neglected few opportunities for fleecing their parishioners. Chapters, monasteries, and nunneries were now practicing usury on a large scale and eagerly buying up peasant debt.[46] Clerics were forbidden from engaging in money lending, yet they managed to evade this prohibition on a mere technicality of Canon Law. No one was fooled, however, least of all the peasants and artisans who, through harvest failure or disease, defaulted on their payments and found themselves dragged before merciless ecclesiastical courts. Geiler von Kaysersberg expressed his disgust at the clergy for "nourishing themselves from the sheep which they were supposed to protect."[47]

Perhaps never before had the Church incited such hatred. The clergy had been ill-educated, worldly, and vulgar in the past, and there's no evidence that those in the early 1500s prayed less, ate better, or fornicated more than their predecessors. Indeed, many a parish priest was underpaid and overworked. But times were different. Seldom had the clergy's treatment of the third estate been so aggressively cruel. Monasteries containing dozens of well-born monks accustomed to rich living didn't scruple from bleeding peasants and artisans dry in order to keep their own larders and cellars bountifully stocked with wine, pork, and trout.

At the same time, a generation of scholars, including local humanists like Brant and Geiler, capitalized on the new printing presses to keep up a barrage of denunciations of clerical shortcomings. Their consciousnesses raised by these humanists, few could now ignore the vast disparity between the current state of the clergy and the apostolic tradition that they were meant to uphold. "The faith is going down the drain," Sebastian Brant lamented.[48]

Now, as anticlericalism swept the region, every natural disaster was attributed to divine rage. In the summer of 1507 hailstones the size of fists crushed the branches, roots, and stems of vines. Even a frozen goose fell to Earth and took four days to thaw. A troubled populace immediately perceived God's flail. And they despaired of the venal, ignorant priests who had forfeited His affection.[49]

In the same year a new bishop, Wilhelm von Hohenstein, was elected to the Strasbourg see. Von Hohenstein was quickly made to feel that allies of the Church were falling away fast. When he traveled from his palace in Saverne to Strasbourg in October 1507, the burghers put him in his place by surrounding his entourage with scores of gleaming knights and thousands of men carrying "good poleaxes, long pikes, or guns."[50] He was being treated like an enemy. Conscious of his unpopularity, von Hohenstein banned anyone criticizing his clergy. He then bowed to Geiler's urgent plea that he undertake a bout of moral reform.

Yet there was a new Pope in Rome as well as a new bishop in Saverne, and the venality of the warlike Pope Julius II was more than a match for von Hohenstein's good intentions. When the Strasbourg bishop boldly threatened with excommunication the canons of Young St. Peter and Old St. Peter, who openly kept concubines in their cloisters, the canons persuaded Pope Julius to condemn their bishop for unlawful interference. After all, said the canons and monks, they were "only men."[51] The Pope agreed: the concubines were welcome to stay. Geiler's plan once more withered on the branch. Around the same time, two enraged, sword-wielding men tried to murder the priests during Mass in Notre Dame.[52]

As he became depressed by the failure of the reform, Geiler's sermonizing entered its darkest phase. He saw demons and devilry everywhere. His listeners left the cathedral with a deep sense of foreboding after hearing in lurid terms of God's wrathful nature; of werewolves and witches sent to torment mankind; of children being eaten alive in the wooded lands beyond the city by Satan's minions assuming the shape of wolves—lupine devils unmolested by an angry God. In a series of Lenten sermons, Geiler warned his flock about the empire's legion witches. A woodcutter added images to his words, showing witches taking part in orgiastic Sabbaths and concocting poisons. Witches can do whatever they wish, even fly on pitchforks, Geiler argued, so long as they invoke Satan's help with a special sign. Meanwhile, in his local workshop, a talented young artist, Hans Baldung, issued dozens of still more macabre woodcuts showing naked witches, their faces and bodies hideous with sin, conjuring up storms, misery, and death. Here was a glimpse of the paranoid demonology that was to let loose more than a century of persecution in the Holy Roman Empire. Like the authors of the classic witch-hunting manual, *Malleus Maleficarum*, Geiler insisted on the need to incinerate every witch. For all the vaunted sophistication of the Renaissance world, the next few decades would see this brand of theology consummated with tens of thousands of fiery deaths.[53]

An aged Geiler, despairing of reform, now told his congregations to take their spiritual health into their own hands, performing penances and cleansing their minds of sin in the hope that God would still grant them grace. They were effectively on their own. Soon enough they didn't even have Geiler. In March 1510, his work barely begun, Geiler died. His collected sermons had recently been published. They would go through forty-seven editions as Strasbourg's faithful sought solace in the one preacher who seemed truly to care about their chances of going to Heaven.[54]

Patience for erring priests ran short in 1511 as yet another bad harvest sent the price of flour skyward. And then plague arrived.[55] City folk suddenly discovered painful buboes in their necks, groins, and armpits, and rashes, scabs, and carbuncles upon their arms, thighs, and torsos. Scores of nobles, physicians, and merchants promptly took flight. Fortunately, the outbreak quickly receded. Perhaps the people imagined that St. Sebastian and the Virgin had interceded on their behalf. More likely the freezing winter of 1511 halted the contagion, one disaster replacing another. From Geiler's old pulpit, his successor Peter Wickgram scandalized the magistracy by talking of thirty-three poor souls who had recently frozen or starved to death.[56] But as the well-to-do returned gingerly to Strasbourg from their plague hideouts, a new danger threatened to engulf them. After more than a decade of relative anonymity, during which he was said to have fought his way across the continent as a mercenary, the serf-turned-revolutionary Joss Fritz unfurled his *Bundschuh* flag.[57]

Under the cover of darkness, in late September 1513, dozens of men in craftsmen's garb gathered in a field not far from the village of Lehen, fifty miles to the east of Strasbourg. To each was posed the greeting and question: "God greet you, fellow. How fares the world?" At the secret response, "In all the world the common man can have no comfort," shoulders relaxed and the new arrival was welcomed into a conspiratorial huddle. The rebels' hatred was not directed solely at the Church. Theirs was a general attack on the extreme inequalities of late medieval society.[58] Yet the clergy came in for particular abuse because not only were they so often harsh landlords, but they were also seen (often justly) as having reneged on their holy duties of providing charity and spiritual comfort. Fritz and his desperate followers believed that they were about to introduce a new world order, an empire free from the power of lords, bishops, abbots, and priests and ruled according to the principles of divine justice.

It was not to be. A week before the revolt, word leaked out and lords and bishop promptly dispatched patrols of fast riders to hunt down the conspirators. One of these caught up with Fritz and two compatriots riding through the Black Forest. Again Fritz somehow managed to escape. But as he fled into the Alps or, once again, deeper into the Black Forest, others felt the wrath of the patrician. It was all painfully familiar, yet as the nervy magistrates of Strasbourg reflected, Fritz would probably be back. One of the city's chroniclers made the following entry in his annual record of events: "Fear of riot."[59] The governors were feeling nervous.

For the present, calm returned to the city. Another

crisis had passed. Cheaper bread, the defeat of Fritz's *Bundschuh*, and a respite from plague ushered in months of relative stability. In the summer of 1514, the brilliant and compassionate humanist, Erasmus of Rotterdam, spent some days staying with his friend Jacob Wimpheling in Strasbourg. He later thanked his host for his generosity, lavishing the city with praise: "I saw a monarchy without tyranny, an aristocracy without factions, a democracy without disorder, prosperity without luxury, happiness without insolence. Can anyone imagine greater good fortune than harmony of this order?"[60] Erasmus had visited at the right time. Even so, many of those in the exposed lower echelons of Strasbourg society, presumably like Frau Troffea and her spouse, would have choked on hearing such hyperbole. Had he returned anytime over the next three years, Erasmus would have encountered a very different city. Strasbourg and its environs were shortly to experience hardship of an unprecedented intensity.

Nerves, put on edge, were soon to snap.

Chapter Three

HARD TIMES

The town of Obernai lies ten miles south of Strasbourg just where the Alsatian plain starts to curve up into the foothills of the Vosges Mountains. Here meadows of wheat, rye, and barley gave way to steep fields containing row after row of trained vines. In midsummer 1517 the grapes were bloated with juice and almost ready for picking. On July 13, Joss Fritz, wearing a black-and-brick-colored French coat and fashionably slashed red breeches, passed unrecognized through Obernai's gates.[61] Here he met up with his agents to finalize plans for a third *Bundschuh*. Weeks earlier, Fritz and his followers had broken cover and started recruiting in these hills. His motley retinue of vagabonds, strolling players, ballad-mongers, hawkers, and discharged mercenaries had carried the *Bundschuh* message far.

Fritz had devoted his energies to villages and small

towns in the past, but he knew that capturing cities was the key to success. Quickly he learned that there were plenty of disaffected city folk on the west bank of the Rhine. Most of the craftsmen, farmers, gardeners, and fishermen who were gearing themselves to march beneath Fritz's banner in September were from within or just beyond the walls of Strasbourg. According to the evidence of one of the rebels, probably tortured by the authorities, they once more planned to usher in a new world order. But by 1517 Fritz's aims had matured into a more self-conscious radicalism. All lords would be banished or killed as the third estate rejected every form of authority aside from emperor and Pope. The hatred for the clergy of earlier plots survived intact: the rebels claimed to have at their disposal hundreds of gulden to pay arsonists to torch the houses of priests.

By now Joss Fritz knew well the trade of the professional revolutionary. He had tracked the escalation of suffering along the Rhine valley. Emaciated faces and the swollen bellies of starving children were familiar sights to him. He remembered the desperate years of 1493 and 1502 and the hungry winter of 1511, and he understood that *Bundschuh* rebels were easiest to enlist following a bad harvest when grain prices spiked. He had been waiting, probably deep in the Black Forest, for an increase in misery before making his next move. The time had come.

The crisis that was to culminate in another attempted *Bundschuh* and shortly after in the dancing plague itself, began with the bitterly cold winter of 1514 when vegetable crops were frozen in the ground. The following summer, rain fell interminably week after week so that in barns across the plain essential stores of fodder were spoiled by damp and rot.[62] Unable to feed their livestock over the winter, families slaughtered their precious pigs, cows, and sheep. In several towns and villages in Alsace, hungering peasants turned on the Jews in their midst.[63] High up among the vineyards of Mittelbergheim their houses were plundered and burned. Several Jews were hurled into jail, falsely accused of desecrating the host. Back in Strasbourg, an order went out for gypsies to be apprehended and their freedom of movement curtailed.[64] These were the typical acts of a people desperate for scapegoats.

Elsewhere, only high hopes for the harvest of 1516 sustained peasant morale. But then summer arrived and the sun beat down mercilessly upon the ripening crops. For weeks, no rain fell. Stems of wheat, rye, and barley withered where they stood.[65] Virtually the entire cabbage and turnip crops dried up and lay putrefying in the fields. In the hills around Obernai the punishing heat scorched the ripening vines. The wine that year was famously rich, but the grape harvest disastrously small. The Strasbourg authorities experienced renewed unease. They rushed out an order: all printers had to show their works to the city leader and a theologian before going to press.[66] Seditious ideas had to be suppressed.

Anxiety and false fears now gripped the region. In 1516, an Alsatian woman claimed that she had seen the ghost of her dead soldier husband clutching between bloody hands his own severed head. She rushed up to him to bind his wounds whereupon he begged her to arrange masses for his soul. Another spirit handed her a golden cup, which she afterward sold for eighty gulden: it was later assumed to have been purloined by the Devil.[67] Rising prices were breeding ill omens. People began to believe every dark rumor. Thousands imagined their dead relations to have escaped from Purgatory. These "legions of fury," as one chronicler dubbed them, were said to be wandering from mountain to valley. At night their spirits were to be seen among streets and fields, running and screaming to the music of drum and pipe. Many of those killed in battle were reported to be carrying their bloodied and mutilated limbs. To the thousands of people who heard of these hauntings it seemed that the whole of Purgatory was clamoring to be set free. In the same year, from the printing presses of Strasbourg, came Johannes Adelphus' *Turkish Chronicle*, describing in gory detail the onslaughts of the infidel.[68] The city's chaplains and priests were under constant pressure to perform masses for the souls of the deceased. But the urgent call for an energetic priesthood went largely unanswered.

As the winter of 1516 approached, the scarcity of grain triggered another hike in prices. By Christmas the cost of grain had almost doubled from two years before and had reached its highest level for over a generation. Few people in Alsace had ever had to pay such inflated prices for their bread. Farmers, craftsmen, and artisans quickly exhausted their supplies. They were then hit with a ferocious winter. The temperature plummeted below zero and remained there for months. Poor families, weakened by hunger, gathered what little firewood they could or ventured into the woods and forests at the risk of being prosecuted for poaching. In the new year, famine struck with terrible force. There were waves of deaths from malnutrition and maladies invading enfeebled bodies. Contemporaries spoke of great mortality in 1517. One usually dispassionate chronicler dubbed it briefly, but poignantly, "the bad year."[69]

It was now that the shrewd released their reserves of grain and wine. Many peasants, already embittered by the Church's attacks on customary rights and crippled by its taxes and tithes, were disgusted once more to see convoys carrying sacks of grain and barrels of wine from nunneries, monasteries, and chapters toward markets in Strasbourg or beyond. As poor farmers and the humbler city folk sickened and starved, the clergy and lords cashed in.

In early January 1517 Strasbourg held its annual spectacle of unity, the *Schwörtag*, when all citizens gathered in the cathedral square to pledge fealty to its governors and laws. Nobles and master guildsmen marched to the sound of trumpets and kettledrums onto a stage as before them were arrayed the ranks of guild masters, journeymen, and apprentices. The city's secretary completed the proceedings by uttering a collective prayer: "May God grant you and all of us luck, health, prosperity, and long life."[70] This year he may have rendered these formulaic words with a rare tone of sincerity. After two failed harvests the magistrates had begun to fear the social unrest that Joss Fritz was busily fomenting. Keenly aware of the danger, the city's astute if hardheaded governors opened some of their granaries and stores. For a time at least, grain could be purchased at an affordable price. Hundreds of pounds of fruits, flour, and wine were released at knocked-down prices.[71] Taxes on pork were also slashed and, as suspicions grew that merchants, monks, and nuns were still speculating in grain, the Strasbourgeois were made to swear that they weren't hoarding goods and had enough only for their own tables.[72] These concessions bought some time for thousands of hungry men, women, and children.

Yet by now many families had defaulted on the loans they had contracted early the previous year in the optimistic expectation of a plentiful harvest. At Candlemas, in early February, their interest payments were due.[73] The detailed logs of debts kept in religious chapters, monasteries, and convents show broken farmers and tradesmen begging for extensions, promising to pay in six months after having gathered in the year's harvest. Hundreds more walked into Strasbourg to negotiate new loans. Some wanted them merely to put food on the table for a few weeks; others were in danger of losing everything to the city's usurers, paying back existing loans at exorbitant rates of interest. Once inside the city walls, hard-pressed farmers and artisans found clergymen happy to oblige. Monks who had sworn to lives of apostolic poverty advanced cash loans in return for annuities or the promise of subsequent years' harvests; they had become slick financiers with all the pity of wolves. Their poor debtors went home with gold coins jangling in their purses. Perhaps for a while they could afford to eat meat for supper or pay off moneylenders and liberate themselves from bailiffs. But such joys were alloyed with the knowledge that if the grain and wine crops failed again, they would face disaster. The next few months were all important.

Through the early spring of 1517 first indications for the new harvest brought some comfort. Then hopes were cruelly smashed. After weeks of no rainfall, on the Friday before St. George's Day in late April, a cold spell froze the young grapes in the vineyards and blistered the kernels of wheat, barley, and rye growing in the plain. Shortly after, the chronicles tell us, a severe hailstorm pulverized fields, vines, and vegetables. Crops were flattened, the vines cut down. The harvest would now fall badly short. Those who had borrowed from chapters and monasteries faced the combined woes of destitution and excommunication.

The cramps and lethargy induced by slow starvation were nearly always accompanied by sickness. Smallpox tore through Strasbourg in 1517.[74] With the city's few hospitals already glutted with the sick, its poorer victims had to make do with a tiny, bedless shelter with a light covering of filthy, matted straw. Then, during the early summer months, terror again spread across the region when news broke that the town of Mulhouse, south of Strasbourg, had been stricken by bubonic plague for the second time in a decade. August saw a large procession, *contra pestilentiam*, in which the people of Strasbourg begged St. Sebastian and St. Roche to intercede with God on their behalf and prevent the plague's further advance.[75] The people had good reason to feel alarmed. Few maladies spread so fast, inflicted such pain, or killed so surely.[76]

Yet plague victims were at least spared the years

of isolation and ignominy suffered by the lepers. In 1517 some of those weakened by hunger succumbed to this wretched disease. Once a panel of physicians and surgeons had diagnosed them, the poor lepers knew that they might never again feel a loved one's touch. Carted off to a leprosarium miles outside of town, contact with family members would be limited to exchanging affectionate gestures from one side of a field to another.[77] They were destined to lead lives of acute loneliness, simply awaiting death.

It was hard to avoid the conclusion, arrived at long before by Sebastian Brant, that God had come to despise the people of Alsace. And now, in high summer, there arrived yet another malady wholly unknown to their forefathers. Dubbed the "English sweat," as the first cases had been described in Milford Haven in England thirty years earlier, in 1517 this mysterious sickness reached Strasbourg.[78] The sweat struck only a few, but they succumbed in a shockingly strange manner. First came acute anxiety followed by violent shivers, giddiness, and fatigue. Several hours later, sweat began to pour in streams from the body, as the victim panted for breath, becoming delirious and unquenchably thirsty. Death often ensued.

From his pulpit in Notre Dame, Geiler had encouraged his flock to see devilry, invited by sin, behind the natural disasters of the age. The Prince of Darkness could easily have conjured up a hailstorm to ruin crops or caused the sun to desiccate grapes on their vines. Yet nearly everyone accepted that Satan's power could never eclipse God's. Everything the Devil did had the Almighty's sanction; the Evil One did God's work by proxy. So there was no escaping the grim realization that God had lost patience. It was a horrifying thought. For without heavenly love they were at the mercy of predatory demons, devils, and fiends.

As the misery of the poor escalated, the Church further cultivated its stake in peasant debt. Under cover of providing aid, it drove the region's peasants deeper into crisis and the clergy's promiscuous use of the power of excommunication sowed deeper hatred in the minds of the poor. Kept well-informed by his agents in and around Strasbourg, Joss Fritz planned his next move. In covert meetings in taverns, meadows, woods, and lanes, he and his comrades whispered of a land free from landlords, of incomes undiminished by taxes and tithes, and of an empire ruled only by a wise emperor. Hungry, desperate, and indebted, thousands found the dream irresistible.

The first bonfire, the signal for the revolt to begin, was to be lit in the hills above Rosheim, twenty miles southwest of Strasbourg, in the second week of September. Having captured Rosheim, Fritz planned on leading his units of wine growers into the low country where farmers and gardeners would join the *Bundschuh*. They were then to take the leading towns of northern Alsace, everywhere slaughtering magistrates and other civic leaders. At the end of September they planned to light an inferno on the summit of Mount Kniebis in the Black Forest triggering the uprising of thousands more on the other side of the Rhine.

After three years of grinding hardship, with Strasbourg's charitable institutions overwhelmed, Fritz's prospects looked good. But in August the courage of a peasant charged with setting alight the houses of the rich failed him. He confessed all to his priest, who informed the authorities. Cavalry patrols were again dispatched to hunt conspirators on both sides of the Rhine. The few who were captured, tortured, and later executed expressed a disturbing degree of contempt for their masters, both clerical and lay. Thousands of people, active or passive supporters of the *Bundschuh*, once more saw their dreams of divine justice and a new social order vanish into nothingness. Fritz himself disappeared again into anonymity, leaving the people who had hoped to benefit from his rebellion more dispirited than ever. As winter approached with larders virtually bare, few beasts on which to subsist, and prices still rising, hope drained away.

With no one else to turn to, the laity went on begging priests and monks for special masses, prayers, and processions. Disgruntled Dominicans even moaned to the bishop that they were being worked too hard.[79] Yet in the minds of many of the faithful the awful doubt remained that the Almighty would not listen to a sinning clergy's prayers, songs, or incantations. So they also devoted themselves to private expressions of piety, doing good works, intoning penitential psalms, and praying fervently at the shrines of the saints. In spite of these earnest supplications, in December 1517 many starved or froze in homes, shelters, or on the street. Each day brought fresh lines of famished, ragged farmers and peasants to the city's gates begging admission to hospitals and shelters. Hieronymus Gebwiler, master of the cathedral school, reckoned that in these bitterly cold months 450 poor travelers had to be crowded into the already cramped building usually reserved for the shelter of pilgrims visiting the cathedral of Notre Dame.[80]

But the hardships of the people of the city and surrounding countryside were as much of the mind as of the body. The famines and diseases of the past three years had intensified a terrible conviction that God was venting His fury on the people of Alsace. How else could they make sense of the manifold miseries of the age? Since the fall of the Ensisheim meteor, warning signs had been multiplying with sickening regularity: the inexorable advance of the infidel Turk, the coming of syphilis, the advent of the English sweat, and resurgence of old slaughterers like leprosy, smallpox, and the plague, not to mention devastating storms, withered crops, strange sightings of ghosts, demons, and miraculous crosses, dozens of strange births, and a new spirit of restlessness among the peasantry and the city's poor. What could this mean other than that God and His saints had selected this region to feel their wrath? Nor were these beliefs primitive, irrational, or superstitious. For many, citing God's flail as the cause of everything from sickness and floods to earthquakes and hailstorms satisfied a cognitive need for certainty and simplicity. But it came at a heavy price. For an unfortunate run of events had convinced thousands that their souls were in peril.

And yet, while terrifying, this belief might have been bearable to those who had confidence in the powers of the clergy to intercede with God on their behalf. What made the situation insupportable by the summer of 1518 is that many had lost faith in the religious institutions that were meant to obtain for them the grace of God. The clergy, so many of them steeped in idleness, vice, and sin, were felt to be powerless to restore divine love. Strasbourg hadn't known such virulent hatred of the clergy for centuries.[81] As landlords and guardians of their flock, monks and priests had drawn upon themselves bitter contempt. Only a complete reform in cloisters and chapters would win back God's mercy. But regardless of Geiler's efforts, there were few signs that this would happen. For the present, the citizens of Strasbourg, including Frau Troffea, could only wonder what kind of retribution Heaven would send down next.

It is unlikely that even the most imaginative predicted the perverse form it was to take.

THE DEATH
DANCE

Chapter Four

THE MYSTERY OF FRAU TROFFEA'S DANCE

It was a week before the holy festival of Mary Magdalene, on July 14, 1518, that Frau Troffea began her dance.[82] One can picture her in the shadows of one of Strasbourg's half-timbered houses, white linen cap limp with sweat and her skirt and apron swaying as she jumped awkwardly from foot to foot. We can be confident that the dancing epidemic began in roughly this fashion. Only Paracelsus provides a name for the first of the dancers, but there's no reason to doubt his accuracy. Although he arrived in Strasbourg over seven years later, in 1526, the first person to have succumbed to the deadly dance must have earned plenty of local notoriety. Two other chronicles, moreover, tell similar stories. Years later a member of Strasbourg's Imlin'sche merchant family discovered, inserted in the pages of a manuscript heirloom, a brief chronicle that described how the dancing plague began with a lone woman. The Duntzenheim chronicle, compiled by the member of another local merchant dynasty, also speaks of a solitary woman who triggered the epidemic by dancing madly for several days.[83]

Despite pleas from her husband to desist, Frau Troffea went on dancing into the evening in front of a crowd growing all the time in size and bewilderment. As the shadows of buildings and onlookers lengthened and she could barely raise her limbs, Frau Troffea collapsed into sleep. The repose only lasted until she had recouped enough energy to restart her dance; early the next day she resumed. Not everyone, or so Paracelsus claimed, was at first convinced of her honesty. Some suspected her of being an old shrew who frolicked only "because nothing annoyed her husband more than just dancing."[84] Immediately before she began to dance, Paracelsus would write, the long-suffering Herr Troffea "had asked something of her which she did not want to do." This ridiculous behavior was her revenge. But as Frau Troffea went on dancing into the evening, suspicions began to recede. No amount of spite would impel a woman to such morbid excess.

Frau Troffea went on dancing for a third and then a fourth day. At this point, says the Duntzenheim chronicle, the authorities intervened. The Imlin'sche chronicler claims that her public dance went on for six full days. Either way, she danced interminably, apparently heedless of the terrible bruises, bloody sores, and lacerations that must have formed on her feet after so many days of near-constant movement. Courtesy of Pieter Brueghel the Elder's taste for recording folk culture and the picaresque, we have some idea as to what the poor woman's dance looked like. During the 1560s this Dutch master witnessed and sketched several women near Muelebeek, in the province of Flanders, who were driven by a similar compulsion to dance. Evocative but economical, Brueghel's pencil strokes show faces distracted, pained, and transported with woe, each dancer having to be held by two strong men to keep them moving in the direction of a small bridge. We don't know what Frau Troffea thought or said while she danced, whether she screamed for help or

Pen-and-ink drawing after Pieter Brueghel, known as *Die Epileptikerinnen von Meulebeeck*. Dated 1564.

maintained a troubled silence. We can be fairly sure, though, that like the poor souls who inspired Brueghel, she was in genuine distress.

Not surprisingly, her dance inspired fear and awe. Most would have been quick to interpret it as a reprimand from God, the work of the Devil, or perhaps the result of a witch's *maleficia*. One onlooker, recorded Paracelsus, detected the wiles of a pagan spirit called Mager. This suggestion of devilry closely reflects attitudes to the female sex during the sixteenth century. Women were said to be highly susceptible to demonic possession due to their having weaker minds and morals. "Witchcraft comes from carnal lust," asserted the witch-finding authors of *Malleus Maleficarum* in 1496, "which is in women insatiable."[85] A lustful nature, they said, led women into committing vile sins; these in turn drew demons into their souls. The title of a book by a German author, published in 1517, could hardly have been more explicit about the culpability of the possessed: *Demonic Possession Is a Horrible Punishment Inflicted by God.*[86]

At the suggestion of the devil Mager's involvement, one imagines some of the onlookers stepping back in fear lest the Evil One quit Frau Troffea for a still more corrupted soul. But, unlike during the dancing mania of 1374, suspicion of Satan's involvement seems not to have lasted long. Most quickly surmised that her dancing embodied a message from Heaven. It was the latest in a succession of signs from above, some of them cryptic, like the sow of Landser and the Ensisheim meteor, others more direct, such as syphilis, which seared the genitals of adulterers and prostitutes. After frantic discussions, the view prevailed that Frau Troffea was being chastised by a vengeful saint. He was called St. Vitus. Hence, recorded Paracelsus and several chroniclers, her sickness was identified as "St. Vitus' Dance."

The Imlin'sche chronicle explains how Frau Troffea's dance marathon in the city streets finally came to an end: "After six days, my lord ordered that she had to be led to Saverne."[87] The destination is clear: a musty grotto and chapel dedicated to St. Vitus that lay about thirty miles of rough track, through forest, meadows, and orchards, west of Strasbourg in the foothills of the Vosges Mountains. The identity of the "lord" identified by the Imlin'sche chronicle is less certain, though it may have been the city's chief administrator, or *Ammeister*, a man of considerable wealth and experience called Andreas Drachenfels. If so, it's clear that the governors too saw Frau Troffea's dance as a form of divine punishment that could only be relieved through saintly intervention.

Almost half a millennium later we cannot know for sure what induced Frau Troffea to launch into her frenzy of dancing, hopping, and leaping. It is likely, however, that her crazed behavior was connected to the appalling state of Strasbourg's population after three years of hunger, wave after wave of deadly malady, and decades of spiritual neglect.

Conditions in the summer of 1518 had barely improved since the miseries of the previous year. The ancient hospital for poor pensioners was still overwhelmed. Typically it accommodated around one hundred people, but by now as many as five hundred desperate men, women, and children were crammed, several to a bed, inside its decaying walls. Meanwhile hundreds of mothers and fathers were arriving with their starving offspring seeking to leave them at the city's orphanage in the hope of later reuniting their families. Peter Wickgram, predicator of the cathedral, recorded that by 1518, three hundred orphans were being looked after.[88] Many more had to be turned away. It was in such conditions that poor women throttled their infants and hurled them into the River Ill to give their older siblings a chance. Strasbourg was buckling under the strain of supporting its own poor and so many from the villages and farmsteads beyond its walls. The more humane or penitent citizens trod the streets shaking wooden boxes for donations to hospitals and hostelries. There was never enough to go around. Wickgram calculated that there were 2,200 recipients of alms in 1518, excluding the roughly eight hundred denizens of the orphanage and the city's hospitals.[89] Gebwiler counted a thousand beggars unable to get work. In a city of only twenty thousand souls, this was an unbearable burden.

Some small relief had come with the issuing of "indulgences" by the Papal Curia to support the orphanage and the victims of the recent epidemics of smallpox.[90] In return for buying one of these official documents, bearing a Papal seal, the laity were told they could reduce their own or their deceased relations' time in Purgatory. Yet even this act only increased loathing for the higher ranks of the Church, for one-third of the money brought in by the indulgence was destined to go toward the building of St. Peter's Basilica in Rome, a magnificent embodiment of Papal power that hardly anyone in Strasbourg would ever see. When a second indulgence was offered for sale in 1518, one man openly accused the Church of avarice.[91] Having been arrested, he was later released without charge after a protest in the city's streets.[92] One official recorded city folk uttering "unfitting, bad, slanderous words." For decades now the income from indulgences had been declining as Papal legates became more and more shameless in flogging their wares. Many of the faithful were further disgusted at the clergy's itemized lists of "sin taxes" that allowed adulterers, for example, to purify their souls merely by paying a fine of five shillings.[93]

In workshops, kilns, and cellars, and amid fields, gardens, and vineyards of the plain, the common people were now experiencing hardship on a scale unknown since the plague years of the fourteenth century. Shortages continued to drive up prices. Never in living memory had bread been so expensive, fuel so hard to come by, or so many peasants, artisans, and farmers burdened with so much debt. By early summer anxieties were eased somewhat by signs that there would be decent harvests of vegetables and grains. Yet such expectations had been dashed before. In any case, it would take more than one bumper harvest for them to pay off the crippling loans they had contracted with the Church or city usurers in the last three years. It is entirely possible that Frau Troffea's family had joined the burgeoning ranks of those suffering acute want while feeling alienated from both God and the Church. Where so many citizens were losing children, parents, siblings, or close friends to hunger or disease, a personal tragedy may well have unhinged her.

Whatever difficulties Frau Troffea faced are likely to have been exacerbated by her status as a woman. We can hazard some guesses as to what her life was like from the better documented experiences of other women of the time. That Frau Troffea was of humble stock is indicated both by the Imlin'sche chronicle's reference to her being beholden to the will of a "lord" and by Paracelsus' blithe contempt for her. Given her lowly status, she may have been subjected to any number of traumas and indignities that predisposed her to lose her reason in July 1518. All women in early modern Europe were deemed inferior to men and were routinely lectured on their inherent sinfulness as heirs to Eve's temptation in the Garden of Eden.[94] While there were plenty of consolations for noble ladies, the sufferings of lowlier women were usually beneath the consideration of the elites. Young nobles were known to prowl the poorer quarters of towns, raping women with impunity. In the domestic sphere they were strictly subordinated to their husbands, having often been wedded in early adolescence, at the behest of their parents, to older men they feared or despised. Once married, wives were expected to tolerate severe beatings, sexual violence, and their husband's adultery, while still running an efficient household. Husbands who spent extravagantly or who, broken by life's vicissitudes, turned to the comfort of drink or the temporary relief of loans at high interest, plunged their families into misery and despair. The agonies were typically greater for women because they were often powerless to restore the family fortunes or correct a husband's errant ways. One of the few freedoms a poor wife possessed was being able to opt for burial apart from her spouse.

Perhaps, then, Paracelsus was correct to assert that Frau Troffea had an unhappy relationship with Herr Troffea. The misery of living with a dictatorial and perhaps drunken and abusive spouse might have provoked a sublimated act of despair. It might also be that she was (again as Paracelsus claimed) disrespectful toward her husband. Many women of the period preserved some measure of dignity and self-respect through minor acts of disobedience, or from a sharp tongue and a quick, biting wit. Others of course were querulous for reasons that had more to do with their personalities than their spouses.

But if Frau Troffea's crazed dance reflected her own profound sadness, it was not a singular event. It is significant that lone individuals had felt an irresistible need to dance before. Municipal records tell us that around the middle of June in 1442 a monk danced himself to death in the cloisters of his monastery in the Swiss town of Schaffhausen.[95] Ten years later, in nearby Zurich, a man entered the Water Church where he danced uncontrollably, calling in his misery to another man, an armorer who stood praying nearby, to "help him in his need and come to his assistance." Similar cases occurred in the decades following the 1518 epidemic. In his classic medical text *Observations on Human Disease*, the Swiss physician Felix Plater told of an incident from his boyhood, in the 1530s, when a woman danced for a whole month in Basel. When the skin on her feet had been worn away, exposing bloody tendon, sinew, and bone, she was conducted to a hospital where she slowly recovered.[96] In another case recorded by Plater, a priest suffered from cramps and mental disturbances followed by convulsions. He then leaped to his feet and danced for days. Other episodes of solitary dancing from the region may well have been lost to the vagaries of time.

No chemical or biological agent known to sixteenth-century Europe could have impelled Frau Troffea or these Swiss men and women to dance for several grueling days. But we can begin to explain their involuntary dancing if we first tackle another question. What could have sustained them through so many hours of intense physical activity? After all, it's likely that after three harvest failures in a row, Frau Troffea was undernourished, if not actually starving.

There is only one plausible solution: they danced in a deep state of trance. Only in an altered state of mind could Frau Troffea have kept up her punishing dancing vigil. Since trance thrusts pain beyond conscious awareness, it rendered her largely insensitive to her extreme fatigue and her sore, swollen, and bleeding feet. Largely unaware of her state of physical exhaustion, Frau Troffea acquired levels of endurance unattainable during full waking consciousness; even the feeble can seem preternaturally strong when entranced. So while Frau Troffea may have been weakened by meager rations of bread and meat, an altered state of consciousness gave her the ability to keep moving day after day. Moreover, the level of suffering in Strasbourg's poorer districts was highly conducive for someone to lose touch with reality. High levels of psychological distress significantly increase the likelihood of an individual slipping, or perhaps escaping, into the trance state. In addition, diets lacking in vital nutrients also predispose some to lose their connection with reality.[97] Both of these conditions were amply satisfied in Strasbourg during the hard summer of 1518.

The claim that Frau Troffea danced in a delirious state exactly fits with what we know of earlier episodes of the dancing plague. The allusion to crazed motion in a Welsh chronicle of 1188 records that the participants first "fell to the ground as in a trance." During the epidemics of 1374 onlookers spoke of the afflicted as wild, frenzied, and seeing visions; the dancers yelled out the names of devils, had strange aversions to pointed shoes and the color red, and said that they were drowning in "a red sea of blood." One Dutch chronicler noted that while "they danced their minds were no longer clear."[98] Another spoke of how, having wearied themselves through dancing and jumping, they went "raging like beasts over the land" and virtually everyone agreed that they danced involuntarily. That demons had infiltrated their souls was said to be demonstrated by their wild looks and their need to go on dancing for, as the chronicler of the city of Metz recorded, "nine or ten days, without eating, without rest." The victims of the smaller outbreak that took place near the town of Trier in 1463 declared that "as they danced it seemed that they saw the head of St. John the Baptist" swimming in blood. They were in a hallucinatory trance. Similarly, the women drawn by Pieter Brueghel in the 1560s wear the distant and divorced-from-reality expressions of the deeply entranced.

We also have the testimony of an acute observer who was living in a monastery just outside Strasbourg in 1518. Otto Brunfels, accomplished theologian and botanist, wrote of the dancers as having experienced something akin to the wild ecstasy of the Korybantes of ancient Greece who worshipped the goddess Cybele by dancing themselves into a trance state. "What else is it but Korybantism," Brunfels wrote, "when, transported by their delirium, they were led to dance in unison without cease?"[99] The difference is that the Strasbourg dancers appear to have succumbed involuntarily to the compulsion to dance. Yet, as we'll see, within a few decades in communities just across the Rhine and beyond the Black Forest annual ceremonies were being held in which people deliberately induced trance in order to beseech St. Vitus for forgiveness. For these participants, as for Frau Troffea in 1518, trance made remorseless dance possible.

Once we understand that a troubled Frau Troffea entered an alternative state of consciousness, we can begin to explore the reasons why her hysterical flight from reality took the form of a manic dance. Brueghel's dancing pilgrims seem unconnected to the world around them, but the trance state to which they and Frau Troffea succumbed is not as wild as it might seem. Nor is it a semi-comatose state in which the brain performs only the most basic tasks. On the contrary, in cultures in which some people are expected, even encouraged, to lose full consciousness so as to make contact with a spirit world, the entranced typically act in predictable ways. Studies of possession rituals from Haiti and Burma to the Kalahari and the Arctic teach us that the behavior of the participants conforms to accepted beliefs and expectations. They dance, lay on hands, heal, shriek, or assume the personalities of named deities according to custom and habit. Deep in the subconscious minds of those familiar with the state of trance and possession, there is a kind of script, specific to their culture, which channels their feelings and actions. And just as importantly, the same beliefs that guide the trance also make the individual susceptible to it. In supernaturalist cultures, people succumb to the trance state because they *expect* spirits or demons to commandeer their souls.

So, the reason why Frau Troffea and then hundreds of her fellow citizens began to dance uncontrollably in the streets of Strasbourg lies somewhere among the practices and beliefs of the peoples of the Upper Rhine valley at the end of the Middle Ages. We might, then, first consider the contexts in which the members of these communities ordinarily danced. Perhaps most obviously this takes us into the rambunctious world of the carnival, where people danced with drunken, cathartic, and restless abandon. Carnival dances in the early sixteenth century were anything but staid. Revelers performed dizzying ring and chain dances during which they swirled in large circles around fires, trees, and poles. At a carnival, people of all levels danced with invigorating freedom and intimacy. One contemporary noted how the dances made their "bodies sweat exceedingly." An English poet captured the lustiness of one of the peasant dances, called Lavolta, which was becoming popular at the time:

A lofty jumping or leaping around
Where arm in arm two dancers are entwined
And whirl themselves with strict embrace-
    ments bound.[100]

Bishops, popes, and Papal councils had for centuries tried to suppress such frivolity. Geiler thundered that it was "the ruin of the common people."[101] Dance might even, people said, expose poor sinners to the enchantments of the Devil. It certainly, they insisted, led to untold bastard children. But when the opportunity arose, the common people got to their feet to dance because it felt so good. Rapid, rhythmic motion was invigorating, liable to give them a transporting rush and long moments of welcomed amnesia. It acted like an opiate on the mind, soothing and enervating. Moving together in time also made them feel members of a harmonious whole. All of a sudden they were less frighteningly alone. Anticipating a carnival, and reminiscing about the last one, provided a vital boost to the morale of everyone but the sternest moralist. This numbing power of dance was understood from the Bosporus to the Seine and far beyond. And people danced not only at carnivals, but on saints' days and after weddings, baptisms, funerals, and to mark a priest's first Mass. Bishops banned it from churches, but in streets, meadows, and on greens passions soared in dance.

During the fourteenth century, dancing had even been a spontaneous response to the coming of the Black Death. Chronicles talk of towns moving to the sound of drums and bagpipes as they awaited the inevitable onset of plague. One contemporary wrote:

They resolved that they should try to cheer
each other up with comfort and merrymaking,
so that they were not overwhelmed by depression. Accordingly, wherever they could they
held parties and weddings with a cheerful heart,
so that by rekindling a sort of half-happiness
they could avoid despair.[102]

Frau Troffea may have danced, her inhibitions
disabled by delirium, in part because she associated it
with carefree ecstasy. Fleeing the horror of the present,
her thoughts might have turned to the thrill of carnival.
Indeed, chronicles from the 1370s suggest that at least
some of the choreomaniacs engaged in shocking bouts
of carnivalesque self-gratification. One of them talks of
how the afflicted "indulged in disgraceful immodesty,
for many women, during this shameless dance...bared
their bosoms, while others of their own accord offered
their virtue."[103] It's not clear how many committed
"immoral" acts, but some may well have sought respite
in hedonistic frenzy.

Yet the mere joy of dance was certainly not the
primary cause of Frau Troffea's bizarre behavior. After
all, there was nothing even remotely pleasurable in
the dancing plague. Chroniclers tell us that those who
were momentarily roused from their trances screamed
for help from bystanders, God, and the saints. While

entranced, their minds conjured up fearsome thoughts of devils, demons, and curses; nightmare scenarios, not fond reminisces of carnival frivolity.

Instead, it is the Imlin'sche chronicle and the account written by Paracelsus that unlock for us the realm of beliefs that triggered the Strasbourg dancing epidemic. The vital clue lies in the speed with which her malady was attributed to St. Vitus. Those who gathered around her, Paracelsus tells us, "soon endowed St. Vitus with the spirit which caused the sickness." And, as noted earlier, the Imlin'sche chronicle records that after days of dancing "my master let her go to St. Vitus-Saverne." Why this saint in particular? After all, Strasbourg contained churches, chapels, and shrines dedicated to hundreds of other saints who might have been implicated and then begged to for mercy. Nor was the shrine dedicated to St. Vitus in Saverne especially convenient, lying close to the top of a steep if small mountain more than thirty miles of rough track distant. Despite all this they opted resolutely for St. Vitus. We need, therefore, to explore the popular beliefs linked to his cult.

According to official Church legend, St. Vitus was a young Sicilian martyr tortured and tormented in AD 303, by order of the emperors Diocletian and Maximilian for refusing to give up his Christian faith. They had immersed him in a cauldron of boiling lead and tar. But he came out miraculously unscathed. Nor was he harmed by a hungry lion that Diocletian set upon him. Instead, it affectionately licked his hands.[104] Legend also has it that more subtle attempts were made to persuade the boy martyr to convert. On one occasion he was placed in a room with "seductive dancers" in order to tempt him back to the Roman gods. Even this failed. Shortly after, he was "rewarded" by being allowed to ascend up to Paradise, dying belatedly from wounds inflicted by his torturers. There was already a shrine dedicated to his martyrdom in Rome by the fifth century AD.[105] Centuries later the cult of St. Vitus had spread far.

It reached the extensive lands of the Holy Roman Empire during the tenth century when some of Vitus' supposed relics were placed in the abbey at Corvey, close to where the Rhine flows into the North Sea. In 1355 the saint's arm was donated to the St. Vitus cathedral in Prague and, at about the same time, he was made one of the fourteen "holy helpers," alongside such healing saints as Sebastian, Valentine, and Roche. St. Vitus was to be prayed to by those suffering from epilepsy, or the "falling sickness," and by women unable to conceive. This dramatically increased the popularity of his cult. Pilgrims, mercenaries, traders, itinerant priests, and the sellers of holy relics carried word of St. Vitus and his spiritual healing powers. It was probably shortly after he had become a holy helper that a shrine consecrated to him was installed in a cave above Saverne. By the end of the fifteenth century, around the time of Frau Troffea's birth, it had become a thriving pilgrimage destination, cluttered with votive offerings in wax, iron, and wood. In the late 1400s, a modest chapel was constructed on a bluff of red sandstone above the grotto. Pilgrims and the people of the plains and high-country supported its resident hermit with offerings of money, cloth, and fowl.[106]

But what is the connection between St. Vitus and the dancing plague? We can begin by noting that saints occupied a prominent position in popular and organized worship in late medieval Europe. In Strasbourg, each guild had its patron saint to whom it dedicated shrines, ceremonies, and bequests. When sick, the city's people would take water at the holy spring of St. Otilia and earth from the grave of St. Aurelia. The healthy, meanwhile, offered up sincere prayers to St. Sebastian against the plague, to St. Wolfang against fevers, to St. Barbara against lightening and sudden death, to St. Valentine against epilepsy, and to St. Blaise against throat infections. To purify their souls they lavishly honored St. Bridget, St. Ursula and her eleven thousand virgins, and the Holy Innocents, as well as St. Agatha, the heavenly protectoress against house fires. Throughout the city, saints' days and holy fasts were scrupulously observed. This was no mere mechanical cycle. Peace of mind demanded strict observance and an assiduous attention to the respect owed to the heavenly host.

More pertinent to the 1518 epidemic, a variety of sources, ranging from chronicles to altar paintings, reveal the existence of a longstanding fear of dancing curses sent down from Heaven or Hell. An association with St. Vitus came later, but during earlier outbreaks of choreomania it was immediately inferred that the scourge was either devilish or divine. The wild dancers of the 1370s claimed to be possessed by evil spirits; screaming in their pain and exhaustion the names of demons and devils. In some areas they also implored St. John the Baptist to relieve their suffering. In Cologne, for instance, during the autumn of 1374, they converged on sacred places, where they danced madly, begged to have their stomachs pummeled and cried out for help to "Lord St. John." Near the town of Trier, in 1374, another group flocked to a riverside chapel dedicated to this saint. The same chapel, the chronicles say, thereafter became a regular pilgrimage site for those with "St. John's Disease."[107]

The identification of St. John with the dancing sickness quickly tightened. When a stumbling group of choreomaniacs approached the pilgrimage shrine of Eberhardsklausen, again near Trier, in 1463, they were said to have "called upon St. John the Baptist, whose disease they said this was."[108] The same belief seems to have inspired their vision of St. John's head swimming in blood. Similarly, when Brueghel drew his *Dancing Pilgrims at Muelebeek* in the 1560s, he could say matter-of-factly that they had "St. John's Disease."

Long before Brueghel sketched his manic pilgrims, the peoples living to the east of the Rhine and upstream of Luxembourg were connecting the dancing plague with the cult of St. Vitus instead of St. John. Why this happened isn't clear, though it may be important that stories of a dancing epidemic in Erfurt in 1237, retold in fifteenth-century chronicles, spoke of the poor children having quit the town on St. Vitus' Day, July 15. Alternatively the association may have been inspired by a popular legend that told of how St. Vitus had rid Emperor Diocletian's son of a demon that caused him to foam and convulse. Either way, the first hint of the shift from St. John's Disease to St. Vitus' Dance comes from Switzerland. Of the three recorded cases that occurred there in the fifteenth century, two took place in religious buildings on or immediately before St. Vitus' Day. Nor was the connection between dancing mania and St. Vitus confined to the high plateaus of the Alps. Directly north of Strasbourg, in the imperial abbey of Sponheim, the aging abbot Johannes Trithemius, every bit as mystical as Paracelsus, completed his chronicle of his abbey in the year 1509. In it he commented on the dancing sickness of 1347. He referred to it as "*S Veitstantz*," or "St. Vitus' Dance."[109]

Further evidence comes from an exquisite altar panel painted for a side chapel of the medieval cathedral of Cologne.[110] This city had good reason to recall the dancing plague. Badly hit by the 1374 epidemic, it also lies not far from the town of Trier. Painted in around the year 1500, the altar piece creates the visual impression of two statues, St. Vitus and St. Valentine, standing side by side in separate alcoves atop heavily decorated plinths. St. Valentine was celebrated, like St. Vitus, for healing the falling sickness. Accordingly, the painted plinth upon which his feet rest depicts a young man falling down in an epileptic fit before two horrified onlookers. Alongside him, St. Vitus is portrayed as a simply dressed young man with the typical iconography of a book and a cockerel. Beneath him lies an image of three men unmistakably dancing amidst heavy foliage, their legs energetically raised and arms joined for support and their faces wearing expressions of troubled distraction. The two paintings form a coherent pair, each reminding worshippers of the maladies that the particular saint miraculously cured. St. Valentine lifted the evil of epilepsy, while St. Vitus came to the aid of those with the dancing plague. It's quite clear,

Altar painting in Cologne Cathedral, dated to around 1500, showing St. Vitus on the viewer's left and St. Valentine on the right. Immediately below St. Vitus, amid the painting foliage, one can make out the image of three men dancing a wild ring dance.

then, that decades before Frau Troffea's behavior was attributed to St. Vitus, this saint was already linked to the crazed dance.

But if saints like Vitus and Valentine healed the penitent of their afflictions, they were also said to be able to inflict the same maladies on those who provoked their wrath. In late December 1517, a weaver had hidden in the shadows of the Strasbourg church of St. Peter and, when the sacristan entered, flung violent abuse at him.[111] The sacristan returned the insults in kind, until the furious, and quite possibly inebriated, weaver cursed him in the name of St. Valentine. The Rhenish pronunciation of this saint's name sounds like the German expression "to fall down," which is why St. Valentine was prayed to by those who periodically collapsed in an epileptic seizure. But, as the sacristan well knew, St. Valentine's name could also be invoked as a curse: the weaver intended to cause his victim to collapse, frothing and writhing on the floor. Maledictions of this kind were thought by some to have awesome power. The badly shaken sacristan promptly informed the magistrates and a chronicler added the weaver's "mischief" to his list of the year's most troubling events.

For his part, St. Vitus was felt to be capable of unleashing the dancing plague upon any who angered him. He too was believed to strike down some of those against whom his curse had been directed, and in the western reaches of the Holy Roman Empire, the name of St. Vitus was often voiced in anger. By the late fifteenth century, the phrases "God give you St. Vitus" and "May St. Vitus come to you" were well-known curses reserved for bitter enemies. Nor were these taken to be idle threats. A law from the late 1400s on the statute books of the town of Rottweil, not far to the east of Strasbourg, tells us exactly what the curse was meant to achieve. If someone "cursed" another in the name of St. Vitus, "the cursed person developed a fever and St. Vitus' dance."[112]

A dread of this punitive affliction formed part of the collective consciousness of the peoples of the region. After the twelfth century, there are no recorded incidents of choreomania anywhere else in Europe. So far as we can tell, only those living near to the Rhine and its headwaters in the Alps continued to think it possible for angry saints to inflict such a bizarre form of punishment. Over the centuries, memories of the dancing plague were kept alive in part by occasional outbreaks, like that in Trier in 1463. Just as importantly, towns such as Liège in the Low Countries and Echternach and Prüm in the nearby state of Luxembourg held annual religious dances to which those fearing the dancing mania were known to be sent.[113] During the dancing processions in Luxembourg several hundred of the sick and healthy danced and hopped behind the bishop through streets leading to the church of St. Willibrord. The ritual went back much further than 1374, but now it helped to preserve the fear of a dancing plague issued from Heaven.

This is why the peoples of the region occasionally succumbed to the irresistible urge to dance. In times of acute hardship, with physical and mental distress leaving people more than usually suggestible, his specter could quickly return. All it then took was for one or a few people, believing themselves to have been cursed by St. Vitus, to slip into a hysterical trance. Then they would unconsciously act out the part of the accursed: dancing wildly and uncontrollably for days on end.

Mapping the locations of the outbreaks of the dancing plague that took place between the late 1300s and the mid-1500s provides compelling evidence for this interpretation. Every recorded case happened on or near the Rhine and Moselle valleys, along the western fringe of the Holy Roman Empire. News of strange happenings traveled fast via these waterways. Zurich and Schaffhausen, for instance, both had strong commercial relations with Alsace to the north. Swiss merchants with cargoes of skins, furs, leather, and coal from the mountains were able to carry reports hundreds of miles down the Rhine of the tragic incidents in the churches and monasteries of the alpine regions. In turn, they could take back news of the accursed dancers of Trier and of later outbreaks that might have been the inspiration for the altar painting of St. Vitus in Cologne's cathedral. The folk of Strasbourg heard it all too. Every year thousands of pilgrims walked and rode through her gates, men and women convinced of the active role of spirits and demons in the world, who arrived brimming with the empire's news and gossip. If we consider the 1374 outbreak alone, the contagiousness of the dancing madness is also very clear. From an epicenter around Aachen, Liège, and Maastricht, it gradually spread out to other large towns in the region: Ghent, Utrecht, Metz, Trier, and, eventually, Strasbourg. It is no less significant that compulsive dancing usually struck in or close to places affected by earlier outbreaks. Thus, Trier, Zurich, and Strasbourg each saw two or more episodes of choreomania. Evidently, memories of previous attacks were incorporated into the oral cultures of the peoples of the region; nothing else can account for the concentration of the dancing mania in time and space. So, when Frau Troffea's dancing had gone on for a day or more, the name of St. Vitus must have been on many lips.

It is almost certain then that her terrible dance arose directly out of this rich but now long-forgotten folklore of a saint who healed and cursed by turns. Anxiety and malnutrition may have driven her into an altered state

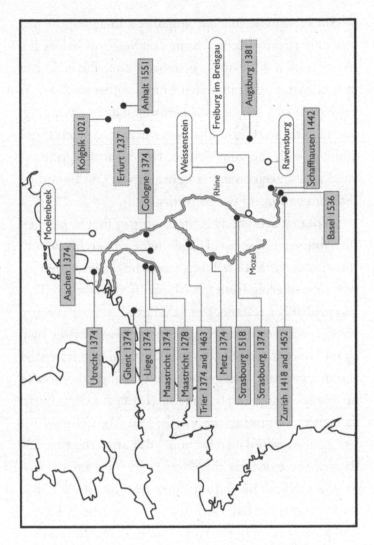

Locations of the dancing mania in Europe 1200–1600.

of consciousness, but her anguished imagination had probably already become fixated on St. Vitus before the trance took hold. It was a firm belief that she had been cursed by him that impelled Frau Troffea to dance as she entered the trance state. Her wild dancing, hopping, and leaping were just what were expected from those afflicted with the saint's curse. Hence, although uninvited and unwelcome, her delirium was still bound by the conventions of the St. Vitus myth.

Not that everybody in Strasbourg at first implicated the same saint. A scrap of paper in the city archives from the summer of 1518 tells of a man who declared that his wife was suffering from "St. Martzolff's disease."[114] This was probably a reference to St. Martial, a third-century bishop of Limoges in France. It's not clear why the man should have thought about this saint, though it may be significant that Voltaire recorded a long tradition of people honoring him by dancing through a churchyard in Limoges intoning the words: "St. Martial pray for us / And we will dance for you." But after the first few days of the epidemic there was no further mention of St. Martzolff, or indeed any other saint except St. Vitus. As Paracelsus noted, once this saint had been identified as the origin of the curse, doubts quickly receded. Frau Troffea was taken aboard a wagon to Saverne around July 20 because her fellow citizens and many of those who had journeyed to Strasbourg for succor in these grim years knew how to recognize this saint's distinctive rage.

None of the chronicles tell us what happened to Frau Troffea. In all likelihood she survived her ordeal of crazed dancing, having prayed and danced before the image of St. Vitus in Saverne. After all, the chroniclers tell us that the afflicted of 1374 were usually cured by ceremonies of exorcism, if not for the reasons accepted by those who performed them. But if the pilgrimage did restore her wits, on returning to Strasbourg a few days later Frau Troffea would have seen her solitary dance turn epidemic. According to the Imlin'sche and Duntzenheim chronicles, by about July 21 as many as thirty-four people had been seized by the same irrepressible urge. Within another week the city found itself confronting the strangest, most disturbing scenes witnessed there since the dancing mania of the 1370s had infected its terrified inhabitants. Pious fear had been building up for years, now it was to explode into the most ghastly spectacle.

Chapter Five

TRANCE FEVER

Paracelsus loathed women. Even in a culture steeped in misogyny, his contempt for them stood out. Some believe it arose from his having been born with hermaphroditic sex organs due to a congenital condition.[115] It's a theory supported by both the shape of his skeleton, exhumed over a century ago, and his extreme reluctance to allow anyone to see his naked body in a period unaccustomed to such modesty. Whatever the cause, Paracelsus blamed the spread of St. Vitus' Dance in Strasbourg on idle and disloyal wives. Frau Troffea had started out to make "a fool of her husband." Soon enough, "other women began to do the same thing, informing each other of the trick." Then they fell victim to "*chorea lasciva*" and found that they couldn't stop. Choreomania was for Paracelsus apt punishment for their shrewish ways. To us this is an absurd judgment, but it does draw our attention to the need to explain how a solitary hysterical dance was transformed into a full-scale epidemic.

Most contemporaries imagined that St. Vitus selected his victims from on high. Well-aimed darts of disease pierced the souls of the dissolute, wicked, and impious. The chronicler and architect of the city's defenses, Daniel Specklin, came to a different view. Compiling his chronicle later in the century, he may have spoken to elderly citizens who could recall talk of it during their youth when memories were still fresh. Specklin concluded that the sickness had spread due to people jinxing one another with the St. Vitus curse, a claim that provides further evidence that the Rhenish peoples had long believed in this saint's spiritual wrath.[116] It's quite possible that the angry or drunken did begin hurling around maledictions that convinced the vulnerable that they had been cursed. What's certain is that a belief in St. Vitus' rage now impelled more and more to join the dance.

Some may have begun with relatively clear minds, calculating that dancing was the only rational thing to do. As we have seen, if one followed the Rhine downstream and then steered west up the Moselle, one entered a region in which energetic dancing was believed to be a preventiveagainst the dancing plague. Why anyone, in Echternach, Prüm, or elsewhere, should have thought dancing an effective means of pacifying the saints is far from clear. Certainly, the activity had religious significance. Worshipful dancing had been proscribed by many Church leaders as a pagan obscenity, but it remained popular as a vernacular form of piety. Did some people start to dance, then, as an ecstatic form of prayer? Perhaps. But it's more likely that the dancers reasoned, in the penitential idiom of the age, that saints would see fit to spare anyone who had already inflicted the agony of prolonged dancing upon themselves. Dancing until one's feet were aching and bloody conformed to a popular view that true penance involved pain, self-abasement, and the mortification of the flesh.[117] Some of those dancers who began to imitate Frau Troffea around July 21 may have tried to punish themselves through dance in the same spirit as the flagellants of the plague years who had whipped their backs raw with knotted leather whips, or the guilt-racked nuns who licked rancid sores, swallowed fecal matter, ate the scabs of lepers, and drank their pus. In his last days Geiler had told his flock to take charge of their own souls. It might be that some of those who now stepped up to dance were doing just that.

If some danced as a form of penitential prophy-laxis hoping to preempt or appease St. Vitus, others made no such conscious choice. Probably the majority of the thirty-four dancers of whom the Imlin'sche and Duntzenheim chronicles speak were affected by a form of psychic contagion. Even people who had known nothing about the curse soon knew enough to fear that St. Vitus was looking for more sinners to feel his wrath. Men and women vulnerable as a result of recent traumas were perhaps most inclined to feel that he had not yet sated his appetite for vengeance. Those who had fretted over rumors of decapitated soldiers back from the dead, of devils, witches, and golden goblets, of strange apparitions of Christ's cross, and of millions of souls bursting out of Purgatory and coming to haunt their homelands were presumably well represented among the next crop of victims. For the many whose nerves had been shattered by adversity it was a relatively small step to imagine that St. Vitus had chosen them as his quarry. And of these poor souls, some were ripe to descend into the oblivion of trance.

That so many felt susceptible to the malevolence of St. Vitus reflects the scale of despair that prevailed in Strasbourg in 1518. Many of those belonging to the urban poor, as well as the thousands of ruined farmers who had fled misery beyond its walls, had already feared the worst. We can be fairly sure that most of the dancers had the lined faces, deep-set eyes, coarse, gray clothes, loose, blackened, or missing teeth, and the stinking breath that spoke of the hardships of the lowest caste. The severe strains of loss, famine, and debt had left them prone to seeing divine retribution or devilry behind every unlucky event. This awful sense of being powerless against the Devil's whim and the fury of the saints was sharpened by their conviction that the clergy could do little to help. As we have seen, many among the poor of Strasbourg felt that for every reformed monk or nun and hard-working, underpaid village priest there were several canons and monks who happily profited from peasant debt and savagely pursued those crippled by famine and dearth. Mysticism and pessimism, each mutually reinforcing, made them inclined to imagine the malicious touch of St. Vitus.

The theme of spiritual despair also runs through the dancing epidemics of 1374. Then witnesses claimed that the poor dancers had been laid open to Satan because they were "not truly baptized, inasmuch as most of the priests associated with whores."[118] The Church had insisted that even whoring priests could perform valid sacraments. It said the same in the early 1500s. But with the fate of their souls at stake, many people wanted more than theological casuistry. Frau Troffea's dance therefore turned epidemic partly because there seemed no prospect of staunching Heaven's rage. The very people to whom a desperate flock was expected to turn in such crises were, through their unrepentant sinning, believed to be a major cause of the saint's malevolence. Surely it would take much to sate St. Vitus' wrath.

And so, because people expected it to, the epidemic of dancing spread. With each new victim, the power of suggestion increased. Every time another man, woman, or child began to dance in the street or square, the conviction hardened among onlookers that St. Vitus' ghostly figure stalked their city in search of sinners. And who could claim their soul to be free from blemishes? St. Vitus, it seemed, would be appeased only when the whole city had been consumed by the dancing curse. The city's leaders would eventually realize that merely seeing another person dance could be enough to precipitate the mania in the observer. One witness told of how "this disease attacked many just from [their] looking on" at one particular dancer "so much and so often."[119] Even if such writers rationalized the phenomenon in spiritual terms, they did recognize that a powerful form of contagion had been unleashed. They were right. The dancing plague was spread not by foul breath, vermin, or dirty water, but through the equally potent forces of sight and suggestion.

Unfortunately, there's no record as to the kinds of dance Strasbourg's choreomaniacs performed. Perhaps they attempted the carnival ring dance, their hands held fast, spinning around at a dizzying pace, people and buildings turning into jagged streaks of color and shade. It may be significant that one of those who claimed to have been cursed to dance for a year in the churchyard of Kölbigk in 1247 said that he and his fellow blasphemers danced a "'polluted' ring-dance of sin."[120] Likewise, a few of the chronicles that describe the 1374 epidemics tell of how some of the dancers "held each others' hands and leaped high in the air" or danced "in circles." Several of these chronicles also speak of how the choreomaniacs lost "all modesty," with wildly dancing women exposing their breasts and maidens allowing themselves to be deflowered.[121] Moreover, reminiscent of the dances of 1374 and 1463 that surely helped inspire them, the figures painted onto the plinth in Cologne cathedral below St. Vitus are grasping one another's hands as if in the midst of a ring dance. Studies of trance-induction among contemporary cultures suggest that if the dancers of 1518 also performed ring dances, the rapid circular motions may have deepened their states of delirium.

Not that the choreomaniacs danced in a state of ecstasy. Ritualized trance ceremonies can be cathartic, reassuring, even sublimely uplifting. Spontaneous trances, in contrast, are seldom pleasant.[122] Being unwelcome, even if expected like St. Vitus' Dance in 1518, they are usually stressful and often frightening. The apparent hedonism of the 1374 dancers may have been triggered by their believing themselves to be possessed by satanic spirits; this conviction alone could have driven them to obscenity and carnivalesque excess.

But such behaviors were far less likely to arise among the choreomaniacs of Strasbourg who were convinced that they were subject to divine wrath rather than devilish cunning.

Either way, it's absolutely clear that these dances were in no sense joyful. To this fact dozens of chroniclers attest. A monk who wrote of the fourteenth-century outbreak noted that the afflicted were "tormented by the devil," several spoke of psychological agonies or "dreadful pains," and one writer claimed that "some of them were driven by their pain to leap into the Rhine and other rivers, where they drowned." We also know that the afflicted of 1374 and 1463, like the lone man who danced for days in Zurich's Water Church in 1452, implored bystanders to help alleviate their miseries. Uninvited and fueled by a terrifying supernaturalism, these trances entailed severe emotional distress. Victims may have offered one another occasional comfort, touch, and soothing words providing a measure of solace. For the most part, however, the minds of the choreomaniacs were drawn inward, tossed about on the violent seas of their deepest fears. In Strasbourg, as elsewhere, witnesses and chroniclers expressed pity, concern, or dread. So terrible had the spectacle become by late July 1518 that the city's magistrates once more got involved. Frau Troffea's wild dance had triggered a crisis.

Chapter Six

OF MUSIC AND
HOT BLOOD

Sebastian Brant and his fellow city officials looked on with rapidly mounting horror. Each day more citizens were claimed by the terrible impulse to dance. Strasbourg's literate few doubtless scoured the pages of the Old Testament in search of precedents, with only the plagues of Egypt surpassing in strangeness the tragedy unfolding before their eyes. Even to people accustomed to invoking the names of saints in penance and prayer, these were terrifying scenes. Yet for the mercantile elite who governed the city there was something particularly disturbing about this epidemic. The privy council that hastily convened for the emergency responded with a mixture of awe and disgust. They called it both a "hard, terrible affliction" and a "nasty" and "wicked" dance.[123] One can imagine why.

The wealthy burghers who dominated the city shared the piety and many of the supernaturalist beliefs of the common folk, but the wild dancing of the chore-omaniacs jarred with their more restrained sensibilities. These were men who strove to maintain a neat orderliness in the streets, squares, and courts over which they presided as much as in the markets, fairs, and leather-bound ledgers that consumed their attentions when they were freed from state affairs. They even had an expression for it: "burgher-like quiet." Calm and order were their watchwords. They weren't entirely hostile to the theatrical; the yearly *Schwörtag* ceremony revealed a taste for pomp and an understanding of the emotive power of ritual display. But the current scenes of crazed dancing were utterly unlike the *Schwörtag's* stylized choreography. In fact, St. Vitus' Dance seemed like an obscene caricature of it. Disorderly, odious, and out of control, the magistrates felt that they had to act fast to stop its spread.

They called the privy council the "XXI" and upon it sat the most distinguished and experienced members of the Strasbourg elite.[124] By the early 1500s it comprised rather more than twenty-one members: ten nobles, twenty-two burghers who had been elected by the guilds, and Andreas Drachenfels, the current *Ammeister*. Several fragments of minutes taken during sessions of this august body have survived the vicissitudes of time, not least the blaze in the Hôtel de Ville of 1870. The "annals of Sebastian Brant," compiled in the later 1600s by the local librarian Jean Wencker, provide fascinating glimpses of their private deliberations. "In several meetings," these annals inform us, "the St. Vitus dancers were discussed." In fact, the dancing epidemic thrust aside all other concerns.[125]

The council of XXI's first step was to consult the members of the physicians' guild, university-trained medical men led by an officially appointed city physician. During the epidemic of 1374, few had thought to ask the medically trained for their professional opinions. One chronicler happened to note that they had spoken vaguely of the dancers having "hot natures."[126] But, largely indifferent to rootless speculations about physical causes, the civil and ecclesiastical authorities from Aachen and Cologne to Liège and Trier had relied on exorcism, holy processions, and prayers to eradicate the dancing plague. Things were very different in Strasbourg 130 years later. By this time it was not at all surprising that the elites should have sought medical counsel. Not only did the members of the XXI have sour relations with the bishop and the various chapters, but these were exciting times for the medical fraternity. Strasbourg's physicians had real clout.

Since the cultural revival of the twelfth century, Europe's universities had been turning out physicians schooled in the highest medical wisdom. Their education involved becoming well-versed in the works of ancient and Classical figures like Hippocrates, Plato, Aristotle, Ptolemy, and Galen, texts that had been preserved and embellished by later Arab authors. Medieval scholars argued that, aside from a few forgivable blunders, the knowledge of long-dead thinkers was purer than that of the present because the ancients had lived closer in time to the all-knowing Adam and Eve. So physicians worshipped the old and often spurned the new (when Paracelsus arrived in Strasbourg in 1526, most of the local physicians were quick to attack him as a mindless heretic for scoffing at Hippocrates and Galen). The sick typically shared the physician's faith in ancient beliefs about body and mind. The development of printing during the mid-1400s allowed for the further dissemination of antique medical knowledge and it enabled some of Strasbourg's physicians and surgeons to win renown far beyond Alsace.[127] It was a clear sign of the prestige and vibrancy of the profession in Strasbourg that in 1515 the city appointed its first official physician, responsible for the care of syphilitics, and that in 1517 the medical fraternity had been given permission to dissect a hanged felon in order to improve their knowledge of anatomy.[128]

In July 1518, the XXI turned to local physicians like Michel Herr, Johann Adelphe Muling, and, perhaps, the eminent Lorenz Fries.[129] They may also have consulted the leading surgeon Hieronymus Brunschwig, though

Fries snobbishly dubbed him a coarse peasant who lived in fitting proximity to the fish market. We don't know if the medical men concurred in their diagnoses. Some of them, we can assume, went straight to the astrological charts they had earlier used to explain outbreaks of plague, the onset of syphilis, and the arrival of the English sweat. As we have seen, to consult the heavens in these times was anything but eccentric. Astronomy was financed by emperors and princes largely because it gave their astrologers the raw material they needed for divination. Moreover, in the summer of 1518, the positions of stars and planets did seem to suggest that disaster was in the offing. Those who gazed upward noted that the Earth had entered into the twentieth degree of the Virgin in opposition to the head of Medusa, when Mars and Capricorn were in the ascendant. Tragedies were to be expected. The "remarkable and terrible disease of St. Vitus," observed a later astrological chronicle, was "caused by opposition to the head of Medusa."[130]

In this case, however, Strasbourg's leading physicians seem to have opted for a physical explanation. After a consultation, the council of XXI recorded a clear verdict: the "dance is a natural disease, which comes from overheated blood."[131] This was orthodox Galenism, derived from the "humoural theory" put forward by Hippocrates of Cos in the third century

BC and refined by Claudius Galen, a Greek physician working in first-century Rome. According to this powerful set of ideas, health depended on the relative proportions and quality of one's internal fluids: blood, phlegm, yellow bile, and black bile. Inappropriate diet, too little rest, constipation, suppressed menstruation, excess work, and one's state of mind could all disturb the precarious equilibrium of humors, or cause one or more to spoil or burn. The disease a person developed depended on which of the humors were depleted, in excess, or somehow tainted. Overabundant phlegm, for instance, could cause mania or colds, while too much black bile might induce melancholy or hemorrhoids. The task of the physician was to identify the offending humor and remove it, usually through bloodletting, vomiting, purging, prescribing exercise, or a carefully controlled diet. These same humors also influenced personality. A preponderance of black bile made for a melancholy nature and an excess of yellow bile rendered one ill-tempered. Most fortunate were those with lots of blood, for they were inclined to laughter, merriness, and the enjoyment of music and song.

One might, though, have too much of a good thing. Blockages in the body could lead to blood pooling up in the form of fluxes. If not expelled, they would start to rot and in doing so, become hot. If this overheated the brain, said Galen in his classic *Ars Medica*, "there is bitter anger and madness and rashness."[132] Most sixteenth-century physicians agreed that excess heat could cause bizarre, erratic, and frightening behavior. This isn't to say that they all rejected the demonic or divine. A few did insist that madness was only ever humoral, but more argued that Satan or God could inflict it through physical means: stirring up the humors, toying with the optical nerves, corrupting the blood. It was common, in fact, to combine the physical and the spiritual. The surgeon Brunschwig, for instance, had recommended that plague victims swallow medicines and apply ointments but at the same time pray to the appropriate saints.[133] Most physicians also acknowledged that some afflictions were solely caused by God or the Devil. They also knew how to identify them: with a hint of conceit, any sickness that failed to respond to their medicines they chalked up as the result of spiritual forces alone.

In July 1518, the physicians were evidently very confident in their ability to eradicate this latest plague, however strange it seemed and despite not being able to find mention of it in their treasured ancient texts or Arab commentaries. Impugning the popular view that the affliction had been sent down by St. Vitus, they claimed exclusive authority, as physicians, to stamp it out. This was clearly a case of vitiated blood, not devilry or possession. Only those well-schooled in Aristotle, Hippocrates, and Galen could begin to understand what was going on. This self-belief was apparently persuasive. Even the bishop's palace seemed to agree. Having been consulted by the council of XXI, belatedly one suspects, the bishop's vicar supported the idea of targeting the body rather than the soul. A chronicler recorded the vicar's view that since the physicians had declared that it was "a natural sickness," it made sense first to "try natural means with it."[134] Perhaps the bishop preferred not to think that the diocese had been singled out for divine punishment. Under pressure from a "superstitious public," some prayers were ordered by the XXI, but there is no evidence at this stage of mass processions, special Masses, or pilgrimages. Frau Troffea had been taken posthaste to the St. Vitus shrine at Saverne but for the most part, it seems that the new victims were to receive "natural medicine" instead.

Yet the remedy proposed by the XXI was not derived from the collected works of Hippocrates, Galen, or any of their successors. Their prescription was simple: more dancing. Only if victims went on dancing, both day and night, would they recover their minds.

If, as seems likely, this reflected the advice of the physicians, it was unconventional medical advice to say the least. Possibly they felt that smoky residues of burned blood had built up dangerously in the dancers' bodies and that through heavily perspiring these might be expelled. Decades later, an English traveler in southern Italy encountered people dancing manically and was informed that they would be healed by it due to "long and violent exercise causing a great evacuation by sweat."[135] Yet these Italian dancers were not the victims of a psychic epidemic: they were performing the centuries-old ritual of the tarantella. They genuinely believed themselves to have been bitten by tarantulas and that sweating profusely would expel the venom. The situation in Strasbourg was quite different. Here the physicians claimed the wild dancing was caused by hot blood. In such circumstances Galen would certainly not have prescribed physical activity. In fact he had made it quite clear that "exercise is more subject to inflame [than cool] the blood."[136] Instead, he would have recommended copious bleeding and a cooling diet.

If ancient authority did not endorse dancing as a remedy, might it be that the physicians and the XXI were relying on a belief in the therapeutic qualities of music? Arabic texts based on ancient learning spoke of the power of melody to restore the harmony of the soul and humors. Several told the story of Pythagoras calming a drunk adolescent by changing the rhythm of the music to which he was listening. In the works of the great eleventh-century scholar Constantine of Africa, there was also brief mention of the healing power of music. About thirty years after the Strasbourg epidemic, the brilliant French surgeon Ambroise Paré explained that St. Vitus' Dance was caused by an "abundance of blood" and could only be cured "through music."[137] Yet aside from Constantine's cursory remark, there is no evidence of such advice from before 1518. As far as we can tell, European physicians were not interested in music as a medium for healing. In any case, they would not have prescribed dancing as well as music had they only been convinced of the curative properties of the latter. Clearly, the music was only intended to facilitate the dancing. They imagined dance to be both illness *and* cure.

In all likelihood the authorities drew the idea of a healing dance not from medical texts but from the wisdom of those who knew something of the dancing plague. Dancing seems, after all, to have been a typical response to the curse. Upstream in Basel and Zurich, choreomaniacs had been left to dance to either health or death. When several women danced uncontrollably in Zurich's Water Church in 1418, a quick-thinking blacksmith pushed back the crowd of onlookers to give them more space.[138] Nothing was to impede their dance. A few days by boat northwest of Strasbourg, the ritualized dances of Echternach, Liège, and Prüm were likewise believed to cure pilgrims of such maladies as epilepsy and St. John's Dance, and Brueghel's drawing of choreomaniacs describes them as pilgrims who were dancing so as to rid themselves of the threat of the dancing curse. So even if the Strasbourg physicians were cocksure in their insistence that they were treating a physical disease, they appear to have acceded to the popular belief that only dance cured the mania. Nevertheless, the fact that non-sacred places were selected for the treatment suggests that they did so on their own terms. They had not adopted a Galenic remedy, but one suspects that the physicians found a way of fitting their therapy to standard medical doctrines. Certainly, there is no indication that priests or monks played a part in the treatment at this stage; the records imply that there wasn't a whiff of holy incense around the dancers. Indeed, one contemporary condemned the decision to allow special prayers as pandering to absurd superstition.

In largely excluding the clergy the physicians and XXI were taking a gamble. They couldn't afford to be wrong.

Chapter Seven

LORDS OF THE DANCE

By July 25, the sickness had seized about fifty people. In narrow streets, squares, and homes across the city, alone or in small groups, the dancers moved with a relentless intensity. For several days the members of the XXI had held back. Now, equipped with the latest medical wisdom, the city leaders took charge. They first issued instructions that the carpenters' and tanners' guilds were to set aside their halls for the dancers.[139] Stalls, tables, and benches were hastily removed and the afflicted were, with difficulty one assumes, escorted inside. The carpenters and tanners were among the least prestigious guilds; the well-heeled shippers, butchers, and goldsmiths presumably weren't going to have their premises sullied by crazed dancers. Then again, the dance had struck disproportionately the poorer members of the city; some of them probably belonged to these guilds. Whether they were rich or poor, the victims soon filled the two halls.

The council of XXI next ordered the outdoor grain market to be emptied of stalls, sacks, and carts.[140] A short walk from the cathedral square, just north of where merchants gathered to sell fish, game, and vegetables, the market was surrounded by stone walls and overlooked by a tower, over which fluttered a flag bearing the red and white livery of the city. In the last days of July more dancers were gathered up and driven inside the market walls and there left to dance freely and without interruption. During the morning and late evening, the market's walls would afford the dancers some protection from the sun. But reaching its zenith at noon, on clear days it would beat down mercilessly upon them.

Just to the east of here, close to the city walls that looked out toward a distant Black Forest, lay an open area where horses, donkeys, and mules were traded. In this broad expanse, the council next ordered craftsmen to assemble scaffolding and construct a makeshift stage for the remainder of the dancers.[141] Amid braying, whinnying, and the pungent aromas of sweat and manure, perhaps twenty or more of the afflicted were lifted onto the stage to perform their wild movements. Traders in leather, grain, and horses just arriving in Strasbourg must have been horrified to see wild dancing where normally hundreds jostled and bartered.[142] It gives a sense of the XXI's state of alarm that they were willing to set aside one of the city's most important and profitable commercial sites.

A "special construction" on the horse market having been erected, the chronicler Jean Wencker explains that now the dancers were encouraged to keep lively with "piping and drumming in the background." To this end, the XXI hired dozens of professional musicians. They took up their positions in the guild halls, upon the stage, and in the grain market and there played tambourines, drums, fiddles, fifes, pipes, and horns. So that the people could dance away their malady, the music went on day and night.

Only exhaustion stood in the way of the victims keeping up their rapid motion. Every so often they would collapse with fatigue or trip and fall as tired limbs became heavy and clumsy. This would not do. They had to keep moving. It was therefore essential that their stamina not give way. Since the dancers wouldn't have lasted a day in the late July heat without refreshments, the authorities must have ensured that they took in sufficient quantities of water, weak ale, or wine. They surely also encouraged them to eat a little here and there; they didn't want the dancers to stop for long, but nor did they want them to faint away.

With the same aim of keeping the dancers moving, the XXI next released more of its precious florins to pay, as the chronicles of Specklin and Wencker both relate, for robust men to "dance with them."[143] The healthy were to help the afflicted maintain their rapid movements. Likewise, Hieronymus Gebwiler, in a cathedral sermon, told of how, in the halls of the tanners and carpenters, guards were charged with preventing the dancers from either hurting themselves or halting their movements. Gebwiler also spoke of a "strong woman" who danced for six days in a row such that "strong men had to replace one another as guards in the job of protecting her from hurting herself."[144] Except maybe for a few hours of occasional sleep, snatched next to stages or on cobbled streets, the afflicted were not to rest. The XXI's orders forbade it and popular wisdom seems to have concurred. So every time the manic dancers flagged, collapsed, stumbled, or slowed, the musicians intensified their playing, and the hired dancers held them firm and quickened their pace. "They danced day and night with those poor people," Gebwiler recalled. Across the city the authorities had created spectacles every bit as grotesque as a Hieronymus Bosch canvas portraying human folly or the torments of Hell.

Day after night, night after day, the dancers continued with their delirious motions. One can picture them in late July 1518, eyes unfocused, faces turned up to Heaven, their arms and legs moving spasmodically with fatigue and their shirts, skirts, and stockings, soaked with sweat, clinging tightly to emaciated bodies.

Amid the beat of drums and the melodies of pipes and horns rose the monotonous tapping of clogs and leather boots on hard floors and wooden stages, together with the sobs of onlookers and the occasional despairing cry or terrified scream from the dancing host. In the confined spaces of the carpenters' and tanners' guild halls, the air must have been filled by the smell of human sweat, mixed with the stench from bladders, and perhaps bowels, involuntarily evacuated. To some, the dancers' performances surely looked like morbid parodies of carnival excess.

Strasbourg's moralists were indeed quick to see this unstoppable dance as an apt chastisement for the wicked levity of the age. Was it not fitting that many of those who had reveled in wild, carnivalesque dancing had now been made to jig, hop, and leap without cease? Some of the imperial theologians who wrote denunciations of dance had referred in just this manner to earlier accounts of choreomania. They cited in their homilies the incidents in Kölbigk of 1017 and Maastricht of 1278, in which irreverent dancers were said to have been cursed or drowned. These stories had circulated for several centuries; in 1493 the German artist Michel Wolgemut produced an engraving of the Kölbigk dance which was published not far away in Nuremberg.[145] Dancing, according to the orthodox theology exemplified by Wolgemut's illustration, was inherently sinful. St. Vitus' curse was, therefore, its proper punishment.

A wall painting in the Dominican's New Temple in Strasbourg had long warned the city's illiterate masses of the perils of hedonism. Painted in 1474 by Léonard Heischer it was one of many examples in Europe of the "dance of death" genre, a stern visual reminder of the inevitability of death and of the folly of forgetting one's soul in the mid of satisfying lusts.[146] Heischer's doomed hosts underscored the association between dancing and sin. In the same vein, Hieronymus Gebwiler reflected on the epidemic from the pulpit of Notre Dame in the kind of sermon that must have been delivered right across the panicked city in late July. Good citizens, he thundered, need to "keep some moderation in their dancing, and especially to omit shameful and blasphemous dances; they must never dance in the wrong places or with inappropriate persons, as when they dance in cloisters and nunneries with monks and nuns."[147] God or St. Vitus had stepped in because the profligacy of the people of Strasbourg had become intolerable. And, warned Gebwiler, if people didn't correct their ways, God would punish them as he had the Egyptians, "and for our obstinacy He will let us sink in a Red Sea of sins."

Gebwiler's pious view clashed with that of the medical authorities, but it was probably consistent

with the beliefs of his congregation. While the physicians may have prescribed more dancing in line with
the supernaturalism of priests and populace, as we've
seen they appear to have stopped short of allowing clergymen to hold prayers or exorcisms in guild halls or
grain and horse fairs. The more highly schooled nobles
and guildsmen of the XXI were evidently content to
go along with the advice of the physicians' fraternity.
Perhaps, too, the wealthy burghers preferred not to
have to go begging to the bishop or his agents.

Yet the nervous city folk appear to have been clamoring for spiritual rather than medical intervention.
Many of them despised their canons, monks, and priests
as immoral, idle, and avaricious. But they alone, or so
Church doctrine insisted, had privileged access to the
Almighty. Only the clergy had the mastery of liturgy
required to be audible to God.

More to the point, aside from the governing elite
and those trained in physic, hardly anyone believed
for a moment that the dancers were suffering from
cooked brains. Admittedly, it was unusually hot this
summer, but it had been hot other years and yet no
one had succumbed to this dreadful urge. Only divine
intervention, stellar alignments, or both in combination
could explain the apparent capriciousness of this latest
epidemic. People who spent their devotional hours
worshipping saints, who patronized their shrines and

treasured their relics, and who knew which saint to beseech for every kind of malady, threat, or inconvenience were led naturally to see this as a divine curse that could only be arrested through spiritual means. Hence, one chronicler recorded, the "poor people desired that masses be celebrated in their name." While a few members of the XXI may have deemed this popular wish redolent of superstition, the council did relent. No doubt worried by a recent increase in the volatility of the third estate, especially now that its numbers had been swollen by farmers, gardeners, and fishermen from the plains, they saw the virtue of compromise. A scrap of the council's minutes tells us that the bishop of Strasbourg promptly issued a call for "the people to pray to God and to ask him to send His mercy."[148] And so, before the altars of chapels, churches, and shrines in late July the clergy and parishioners knelt down to honor St. Vitus.

There were no immediate miracles from either medicine or religion. Each day in late July and early August the city's physicians and officials, along with distraught relatives, were to be seen leading fresh victims to the areas set aside for unrestrained dancing. There they were left to dance, in the increasingly vain hope that it would restore their health. Perhaps in other circumstances the dancers would have come round quickly from their states of delirium. Many cultures have rituals that involve the induction of trance, the duration of which is determined by cultural conventions internalized long before the individual takes part. Participants usually stay in their altered state of consciousness for just a few hours, though they can continue for much longer. In Strasbourg, the victims of St. Vitus expected to go on dancing until the curse had been lifted. Those who had heard anything about previous epidemics knew that this could only happen through spiritual intercession. Not until they felt they had earned the mercy of St. Vitus would they have a coherent rationale for quitting their trance. The obvious thing for them to do was to go on a pilgrimage. Friends and relations, as well as some priests and monks, no doubt asked to take the afflicted to Saverne. Some perhaps did so. But the majority of Strasbourg's choreomaniacs danced on unhallowed ground with only physicians, musicians, and guards to minister to them. Deprived of any reason to stop, many went on dancing until abject exhaustion obliged them to cease or slow down their frantic movements.

Indeed, a strategy more conducive to sustaining and spreading a psychic contagion would be hard to imagine. Nothing could have been better calculated to turn the dance into a full-scale epidemic than making its victims perform their dances in the most public spaces in the city. Not yet realizing how contagious the dancing had become, the XXI and the physicians had made the situation a whole lot worse. The visibility of the dancers, especially those on the raised platform before the horse market, ensured that the minds of the city folk dwelt dangerously on the curse and the saint's insatiable appetite for revenge. They could see that the numbers of afflicted grew while few recovered. As sonorous music drifted around halls and squares, the plague reeled in its victims. Immersed in the seductive rhythms of drums, horns, and tambourines, more and more of the emotionally frail joined the mad host.

According to the chronicles, some of the Strasbourg dancers maintained their grueling movements for days or weeks, only pausing when severe fatigue took hold and they collapsed from exhaustion. Others would have regained full consciousness after a short period of time in spite of the paucity of religious ceremonial, but of these a significant number were prone to return to their mad dance. When their trances did spontaneously lift, however slightly, the unceasing, percussive rhythms of drums, pipes, and tambourines, combined with the sight of dozens of other dancers, were liable to plunge them back into delirium. Nor had the miseries of daily life in Strasbourg abated. Thousands of beggars still competed for meager provisions of food and shelter, every day more ruined farmers arrived from the plains and hill country of Alsace, the city's granaries were ever more depleted, and sickness continued to rob families of breadwinners and parents of their young. Several of the chroniclers who described the 1374 outbreak told of the frequency of relapse, of dancers who recovered for long enough to travel to different holy sites where they broke down again. Similarly, many of Strasbourg's wretched population seem to have drifted in and out of trance for weeks.

Not that all the dancers of 1518, or of 1374 for that matter, were truly entranced. Two of Strasbourg's chroniclers, Specklin and Wencker, both state that there were "many frauds trying to benefit from the situation."[149] This was almost certainly true. Plenty of frightened citizens donated coins, food, and wine to the accursed in the hope of securing their souls' immunity from the affliction. It's also likely that magistrates and physicians were giving the dancers whatever food or drink they were able to consume. As a result, the temptation was great for some famished beggars to try to pass themselves off as victims of the curse and to profit from rare acts of public generosity. There were other reasons to dance, too. Barren women and those suffering from epilepsy perhaps danced in the hope that St. Vitus would succor them, and some dancers may have had long histories of delusions or paranoia deriving from conditions that centuries later would be called bipolar disorder or schizophrenia. Yet the majority clearly danced as the result of a volatile mixture of anguish and belief. A hard core of the deeply entranced went on dancing day after day, and deep into the night; as the less severely afflicted recovered, halls and markets continued to fill with these wretched, demented souls.

Before long, some of the physicians surely began to feel less confident in the dancing therapy. They could only watch, bewildered and crestfallen, as the situation deteriorated. Just a few days after having the grain market cleared and a stage erected outside the horse fair, the members of the XXI appear to have started to rethink the wisdom of the current approach. Perhaps, they reflected, this madness had nothing to do with pools of putrefying blood overheating ordinarily cool and moist brains. Perhaps the people were right: they were dancing as the result of a divine curse. Maybe they had been correct the previous week when Frau Troffea had been dispatched to the St. Vitus shrine in distant Saverne.

As the magistrates debated alternatives in private sessions of the XXI, the city's musicians went on exhausting their repertoires and the hired dancers sweated in tight embraces with delirious partners. One suspects that, after many hours in the company of the choreomaniacs, some of these dancers and musicians also succumbed to the dancing sickness. Meanwhile, the physicians looked desperately for any positive signs. They were out of luck. It was only a few days after the introduction of continuous dancing that people started to die.

Chapter Eight

VOLTE-FACE

Unless a malady was especially deadly or disfiguring, early modern chroniclers rarely committed it to parchment. They were also sparing in their use of negative superlatives. Too many disasters occurred for them to waste their vocabularies on the merely unfortunate. So it's telling that the events of 1518 drew from chroniclers on both sides of the Rhine a palpable sense of horror. They recorded the events of this summer in part due to the perverse juxtaposition of an activity linked in people's minds with the carefree jollity of the Lenten carnival inflicting terrible injuries and in some cases death. What may at first have seemed a cruel divine joke at the expense of the vulgar and damned had, within days, become murderous. Fortunately, some chroniclers left an idea as to the number of dancers who collapsed, never to get up again.

In the nearby imperial city of Nuremberg, a diarist and merchant named Lukas Rem did posterity the great service of estimating the daily toll of fatalities. "In the year 1518, in summer," he noted, "lots of people died of the St. Vitus' dance in Strasbourg. About 15 people died a day." Other observers were less precise, though they agreed that fatalities were commonplace. "Many of them danced until they were dead," recorded Daniel Specklin. Jean Wencker, privy to dozens of surviving records, likewise noted: "Many of the people died."[150] It's also worth repeating the poem found centuries ago in an Alsace chronicle:

> There was a very strange obsession at
>   that time
> Among the people
> Many people started out of nonsense
> To dance
> By day and by night
> Without stopping
> Until they fainted
> And many died.

Lukas Rem's figure of fifteen deaths a day implies that several hundred people lost their lives to the dancing plague. If accurate, we would indeed be talking of "many," for the epidemic was nowhere near its conclusion in late July. In fact, Rem's figure is not credible, since it would mean that more people died of the dance than the chroniclers say were even involved. However, a death rate of fifteen a day might well be correct for the brief period in late July 1518 when medical advice seems disastrously to have prevailed. And if the Imlin'sche chronicle is correct to say that about four hundred people were afflicted, then there could certainly have been several dozen deaths. After all, late medieval chroniclers were unlikely to use a word like "many" unless the fatalities were appreciable. Nor should we be surprised to hear that St. Vitus' Dance turned deadly. Dancing in the full glare of the July sun or in the stultifying, poorly ventilated confines of the guild halls, it would have taken enormous powers of endurance to keep moving for more than a few hours. While the trance state permits a level of bodily exertion hardly known to most of those in full consciousness, this can also make it lethal. By reducing conscious awareness of pain, trance allows people to dangerously deplete themselves of energy and to place extreme stress upon the heart and circulation. To make matters worse, those who flagged were manhandled into resuming their distracted dances. Few had the opportunity, let alone the inclination, to pause in order to recuperate. Nor did they often replenish themselves with food and drink. A short poem found in Königshoven's Alsace chronicle gives us a sense of the remorselessness of their dancing:

> Hundreds of people started in Strasbourg
> To dance and jump, women and men,
> On open mark, alleys, and streets.
> Day and night—they did not eat much,
> Just so much that they could dance again.
> St. Vitus' Dance this plague was called.[151]

Weakened by exertion, hunger, and thirst, the very young and old, and any with weak hearts or prone to strokes, were quick to succumb, falling heavily to the floor or expiring during brief periods of sleep. The bodies of the dead, escorted by distraught family members, were carried off as the others danced on in varying states of oblivion.

Watching from the sidelines as the epidemic claimed more bodies and lives, the physicians surely realized that the hired dancers and musicians were only making the situation worse. The privy councilors observed with equal despair. Within just a few days, the policy of forced dancing had been discredited. A desperate magistracy now looked elsewhere for guidance.

This volte-face is recorded in a small section of the minutes of the council of XXI, dated "5a Maria

Magdalenae" (presumably five days after the festival of Mary Magdalene on the 27 July): "As lots of women and young boys are dancing the evil dance, music should only be provided secretly [i.e., in their own homes]."[152] It was becoming abundantly clear that the intended cure had become part of the problem. As Lukas Rem noted in his Nuremberg chronicle, "Therefore, it did not take long, until the dancing, whistling, and drumming was forbidden."[153] Another fragment of the XXI's minutes confirms the decision to ban the "use of public music to cure them."[154] The authorities had come to realize the folly of public dancing. The musicians and hired dancers were therefore dismissed. The stage outside the horse fair was dismantled and the grain market cleared.

The failure of medical advice probably helped convince any skeptics that the dancers had, after all, been stricken by St. Vitus' dancing curse. They could guess at how they had earned his malice. The heavenly host was livid at the rank vulgarity that drove so many of the city's men to drink beer and pick up prostitutes on the cathedral's consecrated ground; that impelled the laity to dance in cloisters with monks and nuns; that made them get drunk, flirt, dance, copulate, and cavort during the Lenten carnival or in the city's brothels and bathhouses; that inspired women to don fashionably low-cut tunics that revealed too much breast; and that led clergymen to fornicate, brawl, gamble, and to gorge themselves on the finest foods and wines.[155] Strasbourg had become a den of iniquity, a paradise of fools destined for Hell. Depending on one's theological inclinations, the plague was a foretaste of damnation or a last warning to atone.

Or at least so it now seemed to a jittery council of XXI. Their next response was typical for a religious culture rich in beliefs about spirits and the redemptive power of godly acts. It was for them more important than ever that the people now recall Geiler von Kaysersberg's stern teachings and correct their waywardness. Yet the magistrates could not feel wholly free from blame themselves. They too had found it hard to separate the venal from the spiritual, the secular from the religious. Admittedly they had been campaigning against gambling and harlotry for decades. They had passed harsh laws to punish confirmed swearers, blasphemers, married women who dabbled in prostitution, and professional whores who solicited clients on holy ground.[156] But the *Ammeister* had himself held court in the cathedral during divine service, while the magistracy gladly skimmed off the profits of prostitution by leasing properties on several streets to brothel-keepers. Perhaps most scandalously, members of the XXI had paid for the services of the youngest, prettiest, and least pock-marked prostitutes in order to charm visiting notables. Now, however, things would have to change.

To the joy of the city's faithful, for several weeks organized contrition held sway. A suite of new moral laws was passed. The magistrates began by banishing all "loose persons" from the city "for a time."[157] One can imagine the bailiffs and beadles being sent into the casino, the bathhouses, and scores of inns to eject drunkards, ruffians, habitual gamblers, and the otherwise dissolute. They also went to the city's dozens of brothels and combed the streets looking for the lowest class of prostitutes. Those they found were driven mercilessly beyond the walls. Most of these prostitutes were drawn from poor families living in rural Alsace; they were usually defenseless and, during crises, bereft of friends. By the end of July, hundreds of them were seeking shelter and sustenance in outlying towns and villages.

But despite the gravity with which the XXI hounded out the wicked, sensual, and otherwise sinful, they didn't imagine that it would be forever. Prostitutes were part of the fabric of early modern life. Even moralists sometimes defended their trade on the grounds that men who could pay for sex were less likely to abandon unlovely and unloving wives. Hence they were banished only temporarily. Their return, once God's favor had been restored, was implicitly expected. For now, though, the XXI was wholeheartedly committed to purging the city of sin.

There were also new directives for the victims of St. Vitus' Dance. Short of tying them up, it was not possible to forcibly prevent them from dancing. Nor did threats or warnings have positive effects. The magistrates were, however, now convinced that only divine intercession could help cure the already afflicted; they also finally grasped that the curse was highly contagious and that encouraging the dancing only made it worse. As such, they issued instructions threatening that if any "guild member" was seen dancing "in public a penalty would be issued by the council."[158] Remarkably, a scrap of paper in Sebastian Brant's own handwriting, written on August 3, 1518, survives in the Strasbourg archives; it explains the rationale behind this dramatic reversal of policy:

> On the second day after Vincula Petri anno 18: when sadly at this time a horrible episode arose with the sick, dancing persons, which has not yet stopped, our lord councilors of the XXI turned to the honor of God and forbade, on pain of a fine of 30 shillings, that anyone, no matter who, should hold a dance until St. Michael's Day [September 29] in this city or its suburbs or in its whole jurisdiction. For

by so doing they take away the recovery of such persons.[159]

This note indicates that at least some of those who had begun dancing in late July had by now recovered their senses. A certain number simply fell out of the trance state. On the other hand, Brant's note also implies that they remained in danger of slipping back into it. Those weighed down by sadness may have alternated between trance and full consciousness for days or weeks on end.

For this reason, there was to be neither dancing nor music for nearly two months. Well, hardly any. The magistrates couldn't bring themselves to wholly deprive the elites of their entertainments and they had no power to compel the clergy in this regard. "The only exception," continued Brant's memorandum, "is that if honorable persons wish to dance at weddings or celebrations of first Mass in their houses, they may do so using stringed instruments, but they are on their conscience not to use tambourines and drums."[160] The councilors seem to have realized that gentle melodies were less likely to induce trance than the pulsating rhythm of drums.

Shortly after, the XXI issued another notice insisting, again on pain of a heavy fine, that the dancers remain hidden from public view lest the contagion infect even more people. A contemporary official recorded:

> As the dancing disease did not want to end, the city council decided, that families should stay in their houses when a member was infected— to make sure that nobody else was infected. If one of their servants was affected, families had to keep them on their expenses somewhere or send them to St. Vitus. It was important that these people were not seen in public. The council was afraid, that the people might start dancing, frighten, or even infect healthy people. If this happened, the offending families were punished heavily.[161]

Not only rapid, percussive beats, but also the mere sight of the dancers, had spread this deadly compulsion to dance.

A week after Brant had written his brief note the situation still had not improved. An ordinance sent to the individual guilds around August 10 reveals the XXI's mounting sense of alarm as the epidemic failed to recede. "As the dancing disease starts now to be more widespread again," it reads, "our concerns grow from day to day."[162] Maybe the rate of infection had declined after the pulling down of the horse fair stage.

If so, it was on the rise again. By now the XXI took absolutely for granted that the dance had nothing to do with bloody fluxes and everything to do with accumulated sin. This belief did not necessarily conflict with the observation that the dancing mania spread by sight. For, as Hieronymus Gebwiler explained, it was a "warning from God that this disease attacked many just from looking." So the XXI's new directives treated the dance as a moral punishment as well as a moral contagion. Hence it barred the victims of St. Vitus' dance from wearing festival clothes. Only correct dress and comportment would quell the divine rage. The guilds were told to take in hand their afflicted members: "that they be subdued or brought to St. Vitus, and to allow them no sort of stringed music or celebration, no jewellery or beautiful clothes, and also not to let them loose to run in the streets."[163] Any sign of levity on the part of the dancers would only further inflame St. Vitus' wrath.

In early August the XXI concluded that it needed to pay more earnest homage to St. Vitus than it had in the past. Its members probably knew little of the saint or his nearby shrine; as we have seen, each guild had its own patron saint and much of the city shared an abiding enthusiasm for the Virgin Mary. The consequent neglect of St. Vitus, many people must have reflected, could have been their undoing. They therefore sent to

Saverne a team of masons, carpenters, architects, and laborers who were ordered to construct a new chapel. Standing before the narrow grotto in the bluff of rock upon which the existing chapel stood, it was to provide shelter for worshippers and pilgrims. At the same time the XXI commissioned a local artist, Hans Wydyz, to design and build a new altar.[164]

Behind the closed doors of guildhalls and inside homes across the city, more and more men, women, and children were still being consumed by the mania. The epidemic had now been going on for nearly a month with no sign of declining. By this stage, according to the chronicle of the local Imlin'sche family, as many as four hundred people had become infected. Duntzenheim says only two hundred were involved. Even if neither figure can be verified, it is certain that there were indeed many victims. There must have been dozens of dancers already in late July since the authorities had set aside four separate areas of the city for their use. The number of the accursed had then risen further into the second week of August and probably beyond. Moreover, if a certain proportion were recovering their wits each day, the cumulative number of victims must have far exceeded those who were on their feet dancing at any one time. Unfortunately we cannot be any more precise about the scale of the epidemic than to say that the figures in both the Imlin'sche and Duntzenheim chronicles are entirely plausible. Given that the situation was believed to be getting worse for several weeks, the higher figure is certainly the more credible. Either way, even two hundred people dancing madly, uncontrollably for days is a sight more shockingly disturbing that most can easily imagine.

On August 12, official messengers carried further instructions from the council of XXI to the burghers. Their next step was to implore guildsmen to safeguard the children and relations of the afflicted. They were told to "test their brothers" to see who had already been stricken and possibly to root out fraudsters. Burghers were also instructed to dispatch dancers, at the expense of their own guilds, "directly to the saints."[165] Other notes from the XXI were more specific: "guild members who are infected with the dancing disease, have to be led to St. Vitus."[166] The stipulation that the guilds foot the bill for the journey to Saverne provides a clear indication that most victims did belong to the third estate, those who were most exposed to fluctuations in the prices of grain, wine, and meat, and who suffered worst from sudden falls in the demand for goods and services. The same note added that in this manner "the guild masters could stop half of the dancers," which perhaps implies that half of them did not belong to a guild, instead forming part of the faceless mass of the chronically poor. We get the same impression from a council directive telling families with infected servants that they must keep them in their employ "or send them to St. Vitus."

Since early August, dancers had been setting out for the Saverne shrine. Not that they could have made it there without plenty of assistance. Only semi-conscious at best and with their limbs constantly writhing as they tried to maintain their dancing, the journey was extremely arduous for the accursed. It was a struggle, too, for their heavy-hearted companions. But the saint's miraculous intervention was believed to be the only hope for the afflicted. They had to prostrate themselves before St. Vitus' image, just as thousands had already done in front of the altarpiece in Cologne and in dozens of other shrines scattered around the Empire consecrated to the saint's miraculous healing powers.

Back in Strasbourg, the XXI felt that neither the Church nor the guilds were doing enough. Public dancing had been banned, music was only to be heard played with moderation in the homes of priests and the wealthy, and formal prayers had already been said for the benefit of the dancers. Yet the dancing went on. In late August, the magistrates therefore decided on more concerted action.

Having paid for a Mass in Strasbourg's chapel of Unsere Frau, now they ordered, for the following Wednesday, a High Mass and the singing of three Low

Masses in the cathedral of Notre Dame. Thousands of people, mystified and scared, would pray for the well-being of the accursed, the city, and its council before the altar from which Geiler had preached. At the same time the XXI met to discuss other means of appeasing St. Vitus. They agreed that "the entire city should make a sacrifice to the saint" in the form of an image of him, presumably seated in a boiling cauldron, made from 110 pounds of wax.[167] Votive offerings had been common-place since pagan days and could be readily purchased in fairs and bazaars. Most represented the limbs or bodily parts that the donator wished the saint to heal but few of these wax carvings weighed anything like the Strasbourg offering. They were clearly determined to impress the saint with an ostentatious and expensive show of penance. In the same meeting, the XXI made two further plans. First, they arranged for "many" (according to Wencker's sources) heavy wagons to take the remaining dancers to St. Vitus' shrine straight after the singing of High Mass (evidently many of the dancers were too poor to pay for their own ride, for they had neither masters nor guilds to fund their pilgrimages). Second, they appear to have placed an unusual order with the guild of cobblers.

Around August 20, by which time the crazed dance had been going on for a little over a month, the council of XXI spent some hours debating whether to send the wax image to Saverne right away, before the new chapel had been sanctified, or to install it temporarily upon the altar of Notre Dame cathedral. Perhaps to avoid any delay that might be interpreted in Heaven as a lack of resolution, they finally decided to melt the wax into a huge candle and dispatch it immediately to Saverne. A few days later the Masses were sung, the candle was prepared for its journey, and the wagons rolled up to take the remaining dancers to the shrine.

How many clambered aboard the wagons we cannot ascertain but into each there might have been crammed as many as thirty. The XXI had no interest in providing them with a comfortable ride and so would have packed them in tight. Wencker informs us that other dancers "even walked there [i.e., to Saverne] on their own," though it must have taken them days to cover the thirty miles between Strasbourg and their destination, each dancer having to be held fast by two or more healthy companions as in Brueghel's drawing of the pilgrims of Muelebeek.[168] Others presumably followed on carts, horses, donkeys, or mules. Setting out under the city walls, through the Cronenbourg gate and across the River Ill to the north of the city, the city's hired wagons must have made a diabolical sight. Dozens of distracted men, women, and children, eyes lolling, heads jerking, limbs twitching, and groans emanating from parched mouths and cracked lips, as mounted escorts rode at their side. It was an image to chasten all but the most hardened sinner; a convoy of devils or madmen as strange as anything Sebastian Brant had conjured up for his allegorical ship of fools.

Chapter Nine

HOLY MAGIC

Narrow tracks crisscrossed the landscape between Strasbourg and Saverne. Rough, irregular, and undulating, they didn't make for a comfortable ride, least of all if one were wedged with dozens of others in an unsprung wagon. But such were the instructions of the XXI and few were inclined to complain. We know from previous outbreaks in the 1370s and mid-1400s that victims were often sufficiently alert to ask for help and to vent their suffering and dreads. However, those who were at all sensible to their affliction had surely begun to despair, their minds filled with the false fears and terrifying visions of unshackled imaginations, horribly convinced that they were being punished by spiritual agencies utterly beyond their power to resist.

An escort of servants, appointed by the XXI, had the task of safeguarding the victims of the curse.

Presumably they were entrusted with protecting them from bandits who preyed on defenseless convoys and ensuring that the dancers remained on the wagons and didn't escape into nearby fields to resume their dancing vigils. Having departed after an early Mass, it would have taken more than a day for these lumbering vehicles, each pulled by horses or oxen, to make their way to Saverne. Along the way was gratifying evidence, for those few who could appreciate it, of better days to come. In the city's outskirts, amid coppices, orchards, and streams, fields stretched far into the distance. They were now full of wheat, barley, and rye almost ready for harvesting. It wasn't going to be a bumper crop, but it would take the edge off four years of terrible want. En route there were also pear, plum, and apple orchards, as well as scores of market gardens. On cool summer mornings boatmen were to be seen packing their craft with freshly harvested marrows, turnips, onions, radishes, and cabbages from these gardens, all coated with dew, to be shipped to fairs downstream.[169] Maximilian I, emperor of the Holy Roman Empire, expressly sent for marrows grown here for the imperial table. After years of ruinous weather in which countless vegetables had been pulverized by hail or destroyed by rot, the gardens were recovering.

But the signs of the long years of suffering were also still very much in evidence. Many villages across the plain had been depopulated as starving farmers fled to Strasbourg for alms, those left behind in shattered hovels barely subsisting on meager portions of whatever food they could procure. Most of the country folk's livestock were long since slaughtered. Only the monastic houses, secular lords, and some of the richest peasants were thriving in these dark days: those who had been able to sell reserves of grain at record prices and use the profits to advance loans at high interest to pinched-faced farmers and peasants.

After many hours on the road and probably a night sleeping in fields or barns along the way, the town of Saverne came into view. Perched at the foot of the Vosges mountain range alongside the Zorn Valley, it lay in the shadow of a crest of heavily forested hills. From close to the summit of one of these hills loomed the towering keep of the fortress of Greifenstein, a potent symbol of the worldly power of its owner, his holiness the bishop of Strasbourg.

Entering Saverne, the wagons came to a halt not far from the bishop's palace and a medieval church built out of red sandstone quarried from the mountains to the west. By now the people of this typically quiet town were growing accustomed to the sight of crazed men, women, and children arriving from Strasbourg. Over the preceding days, in compliance with earlier directives issued by the XXI, a number of them would have passed through on their way to the shrine. It's not known if Bishop Wilhelm von Hohenstein was there when the wagons arrived. If so, one can imagine him feeling more certain than ever that God had turned away from His people. Perhaps Bishop von Hohenstein castigated himself for not insisting with more vehemence on the clergy reforming their morals. The previous twenty-five years had witnessed an escalation in disasters, but few of them could have been as disturbing to a man of the cloth as this plague of deadly dancing.

The servants briefly left the wagons, carrying with them signed orders from the XXI which instructed them to "choose three to four priests with the help of the local dean, who will then perform masses for the groups."[170] Once these priests had joined the convoy, the beasts were whipped into motion and they continued their journey to the far side of the town. There the escorts must have dismounted and unbound their wards at the foot of what locals called either Veitsberg (Vitus Mountain) or Hohle Stein (hollow stone). The dancers were then carried, pulled, cajoled, or dragged along the steep and narrow path that led several hundred feet up through oaks and beeches toward the St. Vitus shrine.

After at least an hour of breathless climbing, they came first to the works of the new chapel, being built at the city's expense on an outcrop of exposed and craggy rock just beneath the mountain's summit. Immediately behind lay the grotto. It stood thirteen feet high and twenty-two feet wide at its entrance, and tapered gently for forty feet toward the humid darkness of its rear wall. Floor, sides, and ceiling of reddish sandstone had been long ago chiseled smooth. In honor of St. Vitus, hundreds of earlier pilgrims had here deposited votive offerings, including dozens of iron toads left by unhappily barren women and pilgrims' staffs cast off by epileptics hoping that their disease would also stay behind.[171]

From outside the lower chapel there led a series of steps, hewn into rock, curving round to the top of the bluff and to a small monastery inhabited by the hermit who was responsible for maintaining the shrine and opening it for pilgrims. Here the hermit wiled away his days, catching fish from a small pond, tending a few fields, and subsisting on donations from pilgrims and nearby hamlets and villages.

The dancers were now led into the hermit's chapel where, upon an altar illuminated by candles, lay a richly colored fifteenth-century wood carving celebrating the legend of St. Vitus. As in other shrines of the Holy Roman Empire, the boy martyr was pictured immersed in the cauldron of boiling lead and tar in which he had been plunged by order of Emperor Diocletian and from which he emerged miraculously unharmed. The chapel's carving depicted him praying in his cauldron to the left of the Virgin Mary who cradled a suckling Christ Child. To the Virgin's right sat the somewhat corpulent figure of Pope Marcellus I, a near-contemporary of Vitus who had sought to restore the authority of the Christian Church following Diocletian's persecutions; Marcellus had later been canonized as well. Such a grouping of divine figures promised to harness the most powerful heavenly intermediaries.

Here in the chapel there also stood a miniature figurine of St. Vitus, again sitting in a boiling cauldron, alongside statues of St. Christopher, St. Anthony, and St. Sebastian, all richly gilded in silver. For decades, they had been mute witnesses to ritualized displays of suffering. Innumerable pilgrims had journeyed from across the Holy Roman Empire to genuflect and pray before these icons. On August 25, or thereabouts, it was the turn of Strasbourg's choreomaniacs to be led before the shrine's sacred images and beg humbly for the forgiveness of St. Vitus.

The chronicles of both Specklin and Wencker tell us that as the dancers assembled before the shrine, the Saverne priests did something very unconventional. The accursed were given, says Specklin, "small crosses and red shoes and a Mass was said for them."[172] Red shoes. One searches the traditions of the medieval Church in vain for other instances of red shoes being given to the

penitent. And fifty or more pairs represented no ordinary purchase. Whether the red dye had been obtained
from crushed insects, madder roots, or plant leaves, it
was among the most expensive on the market. That's
why the rich wore red garments and slippers with such
conspicuous pride and why only the most generously
patronized artists could afford more than a few dashes
of red in their paintings. It's also why, back in 1517,
Joss Fritz had worn red pantaloons; as Fritz doubtless knew, few articles of clothing were more likely
to inspire respect and admiration among the poor. If
artists of the period, including Brueghel, did sometimes
show peasants wearing red boots, shorts, or hose, this
reflected their aesthetic taste rather than a commit-
ment to realism, as the lower orders seldom wore
anything but grays and browns. Red was no ordinary
color.[173] So it would have taken time and a significant
amount of money to prepare these shoes for the dozens
of dancers transported to the Saverne shrine. For this
reason we can assume that they had been brought on
the wagons from Strasbourg and manufactured by the
city's cobblers. We can be more certain still that they
carried a heavy significance for the priests who were to
perform the rites and for the dancers themselves.

This was an age in which symbols were so much
more than mere metaphors, when religious objects
bore mystical meaning and when no one simply handed

out free footwear. The shoes were somehow meant to assist the healing of the tortured dancers. Indeed, there survives a Latin blessing that was intoned during the preparation of the holy water that was, Specklin relates, "besprinkled" on the shoes. God's assistance was requested so that the water "might prove a health-bringing cure for mankind and that in the name of the Lord and with His blessing and with the help of St. Vitus and St. Marcellus everybody sprinkled with it or everybody drinking it might recover bodily health and spiritual safety."[174] The priests also dipped their hands into a consecrated mixture of oil and balsam, called a chrism, and smudged the sign of the cross on the "upside and downside" of each person's shoes.

One can perhaps understand why the XXI decided to provide shoes for those cursed by St. Vitus. After all, ceaselessly moving feet and legs were the most obvious symptom of the dancing plague. But why did the priests select so expensive a color as red? It may be significant that this color is woven throughout the long history of the dancing plague. In 1374 many of the delirious dancers "could not abide the sight of red" and said they would tear to pieces anyone wearing any garments of this color or pointed shoes. Some also imagined themselves to be drowning in a river of blood. There is also evidence that, in spite of the general aversions to everything red, some of the dancers inexplicably wore pink hats.[175] The color red recurs in accounts of the smaller epidemic that took place in 1463. When the crowd of those ailing from "St. John's Dance" approached a shrine near Trier, they claimed to be unable to see the color red. Paradoxically they also said they could see the head of St. John the Baptist floating in blood. The theme of red even appears in an account relating to the 1530s, by the physician Felix Plater, of a woman dancing herself close to death in Basel. Plater tells us that magistrates appointed two strong men to help her dance, both of whom were dressed in red clothes with white feathers in their caps.

Does the handing out of red shoes in August 1518 somehow tie together earlier and later cases of dancing mania?[176] Might it not suggest the existence of a popular cult of entranced dancing in honor of St. Vitus of which all other traces have now vanished? Perhaps, but unlikely. There's no hint in the Strasbourg chronicles or council minutes that the dancers deliberately cultivated their trance states. On the contrary, everything suggests that the dancing plague excited only fear and dread and that it spread by contagion rather than religious conversion. Moreover, all episodes of choreomania involved aversions to specific objects and violent reactions to certain colors, not all of which are mysterious. The hatred of pointed shoes in 1374, for example, is easy to explain. In the minds of the pious, pointed shoes were symbols of vanity and worldliness; the flagellants had also targeted these poulaines as having provoked divine wrath and helped bring about the Black Death. But the horror excited by color is not so simply accounted for. The color red can of course be highly evocative. For the early moderns it symbolized mortal blood, the fiery red hair of Mary Magdalene, the blood of Christ, even the denizens of the underworld. It was also on occasion linked to St. Vitus himself. A painting of the saint in a church just east of the Black Forest shows him wearing knee-high red boots, a red crown, and fur-trimmed red gown.

But there may be a more straightforward explanation for the handing out of red shoes. As we have seen, St. Vitus' most legendary trial of faith involved his standing waist-deep in boiling lead and tar. Representations of the story accordingly often show red flames lapping the base of the cauldron. Perhaps, then, the dancers' frantic movements created the impression of people attempting to keep their legs and feet from burning as if they too were poised above a fire. If so, the red shoes may have linked the dancing plague with St. Vitus' fiery torments in a way intended to elicit the saint's pity or to invoke his spiritual power. Unfortunately, we'll probably never know for sure. The rationale for the wearing of red shoes has disappeared alongside so much of the esoteric symbolism of late medieval theology.

The dancers, their feet now enclosed in red shoes damp with holy water and oil, were divided into three groups. To each, servants and a priest were assigned and in turn they heard Mass conducted by the Saverne clerics. Every part of the ceremony was heavily laden with mystical import. The XXI's directions stipulated that "the unfortunate people should be led around the altar."[177] Circular motion had special significance to many late medieval Europeans, calling to mind the sublimely circular orbits that the planets were said to trace through the cosmos and the movement of the sun around the Earth. Circling the altar was also said to purify the soul and purge it of demons. The ritual had particular resonance for the Strasbourg dancers because they were being led around the carved trinity of Marcellus, Mary, and Vitus atop the altar.

The official instructions from the XXI also spoke of the need for "each of the sick persons to sacrifice a penny" at the altar.[178] Special provision was made for the very poor: "If the person cannot do this on his own, the one who leads them around the altar should donate the penny." The ceremony ended with a final act of contrition. The dancers were recommended to "donate one penny in the offertory box," which could then be distributed to the "poor people" of the region. This done, they were escorted out of the chapel, down the steps, past the grotto and lower chapel, and then back onto the wagons at the base of the mountain. It only remained to see if the saint was appeased.

Were the pilgrims conscious of the ceremony performed for their benefit in the St. Vitus chapel? Some were certainly fully alert to their surroundings. Any in mild trances or those who had joined the convoy because they feared a relapse, as well as those seeking divine help for other disorders like epilepsy and infertility, were obviously able to offer up prayers and beseech the saint for his mercy. Dancing or walking around the altar, they hoped to feel a sudden surge of divine grace release them from their troubles. In contrast, those still deep in trance may have been only dimly aware of the proceedings. Yet it's likely that the healing prayers still penetrated their states of delirium. This we can infer from the effectiveness of religious intervention in other cases of entranced delusions. The dancers of 1374, for example, were often cured, whether spontaneously or gradually, by priests performing exorcism rituals. At the altar of the Church of St. Mary, in Liège, priests forced open mouths and yelled into them: "Praise the true God, praise the Holy Ghost; get thee hence, thou damned and foredoomed spirit."[179] The chroniclers agree that many dancers swiftly recovered their senses. Others were healed at special ceremonies held in churches and chapels throughout the Rhineland.

Medieval and early modern writers recorded

hundreds of similar "miracles" involving those who had succumbed to a state of spirit possession in which they spoke in strange tongues and assumed the personas of devils and demons. These hapless individuals were frequently brought back to relative normality through religious intervention. In such cases the priests' holy water and ritual incantations worked because the tormented souls who fell into possession trances believed that religious ceremonials would banish the devilish spirits that appeared to have possessed them. In many cases the flattering attentions of priests also briefly lifted the misery that had so often precipitated the hysterical trance. The large number of people who recovered through the power of religious suggestion reveals that even when self-awareness is impaired, our minds can still receive, process, and respond to appropriate external stimuli.

But did the visit to St. Vitus' shrine in 1518 have the same capacity to restore the dancers' reason as the exorcisms of 1374? The answer is probably "yes." If late medieval peoples believed implicitly in the terrible fury of heavenly spirits, they accepted equally the redemptive qualities of penance, pilgrimage, and prayer. In consequence, healing shrines were scattered across the empire. Many arose from popular local cults, built on the sites of "miraculous" cures or sightings of the Virgin or a popular saint. Senior clergy occasionally intervened to stamp out cults and demolish shrines, especially if they savored of the pagan worship of trees, bushes, or glades.[180] Many, though, were enthusiastically sanctioned by the Church. The "miracle books" they kept, to record apparently wondrous cures, suggest that sick pilgrims went there in confident expectation of being healed of maladies that the physicians and apothecaries could not touch. In southern Bavaria, for example, the insane were often taken to a chapel where a relic from the head of St. Anastasia was placed on their own troubled heads.[181] Strasbourg's dancers had likewise been failed by their physicians. Then again, they had succumbed to the compulsion to dance in large part due to a belief that they had been cursed by St. Vitus. From the start they saw the plague as divine in origin and they knew that only heavenly mercy could mitigate what God and His saints had inflicted. For the most severely affected, therefore, recovery depended on their feeling convinced that they had done enough for the saint to lift his curse. The power of suggestion had induced the trance, but it could also bring them back to normality.

Everything about the pilgrimage to Saverne promised a positive outcome: the excruciating journey from Strasbourg by wagon; the grueling climb to a remote hermit's monastery high above the Alsatian plain; the wearing of sacred shoes; an atmosphere in the chapel charged with Latin prayers and incantations, thick with the scent of incense and the smoke of guttering candles; and a chapel replete with holy relics, religious images, and the clutter of votive offerings that denoted a healing shrine. This elaborate ritual spoke directly and clearly to their mystical piety. They at last had reason to believe that the curse would be raised. We can therefore probably take the chronicler Specklin at his word when he informs us that the pilgrimage to Saverne "helped most of them."[182]

In addition to the psychological effect of the healing ritual itself, the choreomaniacs had another reason to recover and to remain free from the St. Vitus curse, at least for a time. Many of them had experienced years of neglect, misery, want, and exploitation, but in the previous days or weeks they had been subject to the earnest attentions of civic and religious leaders who would normally have treated them with unmitigated contempt. To many of the alienated and the marginalized, the response of the authorities must have felt deeply gratifying. Reflecting on the assiduity with which Church and government had sought to cure their ills, many were emotionally fortified against a relapse.

Chapter Ten

AFTERMATH

In the days and weeks after the pilgrimage to the St. Vitus shrine, the dancing epidemic did indeed come to a halt. It didn't disappear overnight. From his palace in Saverne, Bishop von Hohenstein issued instructions for a hostel to be built not far from the shrine to accommodate those suffering from *"morbus sancti Viti vulgariter."*[183] By then, word had spread of the miraculous cures brought about before the carving of Vitus, Mary, and Marcellus. So, for a while, Saverne was probably deluged by people with all manner of maladies making the trek up to grotto and chapel. However, the hostel requested by the bishop was never constructed. It no longer seemed necessary. Across the plain in Strasbourg, the number of those affected by the dancing plague was reduced to a trickle.

Then there were none at all.

As the farmers and vine growers of the region filled their carts and barrels with decent harvests of grain and grapes, the epidemic simply faded away. The acute terror of the saint's curse had at last lifted. Nevertheless, those who had regained their reason would have been slow to forget their recent madness. It had been a deeply traumatic experience, and for many, complete recovery might have taken decades or more. Like the children who were said to have danced out of the town of Erfurt in 1237, some of the survivors were probably left with such nervous symptoms as twitches, shakes, tics, anxiety, and insomnia for years to come. One imagines that many of them afterward led more penitent lives, worshipping the saint whose wrath it was believed they had so painfully incurred.

As the crisis passed, Strasbourg's magistrates returned to their neglected administrative and commercial affairs. Prohibitions against public dancing and the playing of drums, horns, and tambourines came to an end late in September. It wasn't long before the casino was flourishing, while tight hose, low-cut bodices, short jackets, and fancy slippers were soon back in vogue. The brothels and bathhouses also reopened. The more incorrigible priests and monks invited concubines back to their cells. Not that the events of the summer were forgotten. The Saverne shrine continued to enjoy a surge in popularity. On June 15, 1519, the festival of St. Vitus, parties of worshippers, some presumably from Strasbourg itself, trudged up the Vitus Mountain to worship before his images. The inhabitants of parishes closer to Saverne carried aloft banners and left offerings on the altar and in the poor box as the choreomaniacs had done before them.

The years immediately after 1518 brought further respite to the impoverished farmers, artisans, wine makers, and peasants whose misery had fueled the dancing epidemic. Several good harvests probably restored their confidence in God's benevolent presence.[184] Perhaps just as importantly, a brief period of heady optimism now dawned as the region began to feel the force of religious reformation. Word reached the city in late 1518 that Martin Luther, a previously obscure Augustinian friar from the imperial city of Wittenberg, had accused the Papacy of venality in selling indulgences for its own enrichment. By 1521, Strasbourg's popular preacher, Matthäus Zell, was openly and dangerously defending Luther's theology. Zell's sermons infuriated Bishop von Hohenstein and the city chapters, but the populace that had long resented the clergy's failure to live by city laws, to pay its taxes, or contribute toward its defense, now listened avidly to the propagators of Luther's ideas.[185] The reformers insisted that grace could come only as a gift from God, not through costly penances or indulgences sold by the Church. Christ's message had been obscured, they added, by centuries of false theology. As a result believers must read the Bible for themselves, rejecting the authority of that "kingly priesthood" of popes and bishops. Many among the ranks of Strasbourg's poor realized that this new brand of theology promised to bring an end to tithes, ecclesiastical fines, and the clergy's financial stranglehold on the city. Luther's doctrines sounded so refreshingly egalitarian. All this talk of a gluttonous clergy being replaced by a "priesthood of all believers" reminded many of the *Bundschuh*'s heady goal of equality on Earth.

Hence the members of Strasbourg's small trades flocked to the cause: clothiers, woolworkers, metalworkers, masons, stonemasons, fishermen, and gardeners. In 1521 hundreds of them broke into a Carthusian monastery and gorged themselves on excellent food and wine. Later, when canons tried to sell indulgences in the chapter of Young St. Peter, the money from the indulgence coffer was seized and poured into the alms box. The pent up frustrations and resentments that had surfaced bizarrely in the summer of 1518 were heading for more conventional expression. In Luther's pamphlets and from popular preachers, the Empire's poor were shortly to find justification for what was to be the largest rebellion of the common man before the French Revolution.

Across the region, peasants and artisans began to feel that the time had come to realize Joss Fritz's *Bundschuh* dream. Fritz himself, now a gray-haired veteran, was seen in 1525 helping to prepare for rebellion in the Black Forest. Old grievances about the attacks by lords and clergy on ancient rights of grazing, fishing, and foraging, and anger at escalating taxes and the introduction of serfdom, were fused with and focused by deep-seated anticlericalism, sparking violent revolt throughout the southern, central, and western regions of the Holy Roman Empire. Contemporary reports suggest the involvement of an extraordinary 300,000 peasants.[186] The countryside around Strasbourg was quickly engulfed, while many of the city's gardeners and hand workers downed tools, quit the city, and joined armed bands in looting and sacking convents across the Alsatian plain. For weeks they terrorized nuns and priests, exulting in the turning of tables so chillingly predicted in the apocalyptic *Reformation of Sigismund.*

This bout of vengeful violence could not last. On May 16, 1525, the magistrates of Strasbourg received a letter composed earlier in the day. It told them that among a 15,000-strong peasant army, waiting within the thick defensive walls of Saverne, were hundreds of men from their city. "Look at your poor citizens, and the fruit of our land," the rebel captain shakily wrote, "that you may do right and not abandon us completely." In more plaintive tone the letter went on: "Do it for God's sake; come, help us." Poignantly he concluded: "Given in fear at Saverne." Just three hours later, the captain wrote again, his hand doubtless shaking as doom, in the form of thousands of disciplined troops under the command of the duke of Lorraine, approached from across the plain: "Oh, you Christian lords, we pray to you as your children and citizens, do not abandon us in our distress and misery." Three hours later the duke arrived, bringing carnage and the din of battle. In an orgy of killing, his troops ruthlessly cut down the peasant horde. They then turned on the townspeople, even destroying the bishop's palace. Several hundred ill-clad corpses had to be stacked up and burned.

In many parts of the empire lords, bishops, and knights exacted a brutal vengeance. The magistrates of Strasbourg, in contrast, acted with a burgher-like moderation. Troubled by the disorder of previous years, perhaps even sympathetic to the plight of the city's destitute, the Strasbourg elites set about reforming the dispensing of charity. From his pulpit in Notre Dame, Geiler had long ago implored them to introduce new regulations to assist the genuinely needy in their homes rather than forcing them to beg in the city streets.[187] In the wake of the Peasant's War, the XXI passed just such an ordinance. From now on the unfortunate would be cared for by the city, from publicly collected alms and benefactions confiscated from the Catholic Church. This new policy certainly eased the plight of some of the poor, but it was no panacea. Indeed, there would be many more hard times for the peasants and artisans of Alsace in the coming decades. The year 1531, for instance, would see a disastrous harvest and usher in grain prices even higher than those during the bitter winter of 1517. Yet when famine and disease struck again, the humbler people of Strasbourg and its environs were at least spared one of the many torments of the recent past: the dancing plague.

So far as we can tell, St. Vitus' curse never came back to terrorize the inhabitants of Strasbourg. After 1518 there are no further records of the dancing plague afflicting those living in or around the city. Curiously this may have had at least something to do with the advent of the Protestant Reformation. For as they turned on the priests, canons, and monks in their midst, Strasbourg's poor were rejecting many of the traditional beliefs and practices of the medieval Church. Luther had condemned the veneration of saints and the Virgin as pagan perversions. Under his influence, the myriad images of saints that were carved into façades and pulpits or placed in alcoves and on altars came to stand for the old Church, its corruption, worldliness, and greed. The same challenge to medieval piety was visible across much of the Empire where, for a generation, fewer and fewer people set out on pilgrimages to healing shrines. When Strasbourg's third estate allied itself with the Lutheran preachers, its members directed their fury at the shrines, sculptures, altar pieces, and relics before which they had once genuflected and prayed. In 1524, an angry mob burst into Young St. Peter and proceeded to pulverize its statuary.[188] Later in the same year, members of the gardeners' guild pillaged and smashed the tomb of St. Aurelie. While attacking the ancient tradition of saint worship, they were undercutting belief in the powers of saints to heal and curse. For as long as people followed Luther in condemning the devotion to saints' cults, they were to some degree protected against renewed bouts of the St. Vitus madness.

Elsewhere the survival of traditional practices and beliefs kept the dancing mania alive. Felix Plater's *Observations on Human Disease* tells, as noted earlier, of a Swiss woman who danced for a whole month and a priest who danced for several days. Another example is recorded in a collection of stories published in 1572. It relates the case of three children, from the same family, who in 1551 danced, leapt, snorted, and writhed day after day in the principality of Anhalt, pausing only to eat and sleep for short periods. The author of the account, Hondorff, recorded that the priest's attempts at exorcism failed.[189] Many similar incidents were probably never committed to paper, or if they were the records have been lost.

Much more intriguing, however, are later reports of the deliberate inducement of St. Vitus' Dance in the northern province of Flanders as well as in several imperial territories close to Strasbourg itself: Swabia, Freiburg im Breisgau, and Ulm. The first evidence of fully fledged possession cults having grown up around the alleged healing powers of St. John or St. Vitus comes from the pencil of Brueghel. In Moelenbeek, in Flanders, an annual dance was being performed in the mid-1500s. A line of women, and the occasional man, danced in delirium to the music of bagpipes toward the Church of St. John. In 1564, Brueghel drew these pilgrims, adding a note explaining that having "danced over a bridge and hopped a great deal they will be cleansed for a whole year of St. John's disease."[190] These people wanted to suffer from the dance frenzy for a day, apparently believing that for doing so St. John would relieve them of the curse for the remainder of the year.[191] By implication, they repeated the performance year after year.

Similarly, in 1609 the physician Schenk von Grafenberg wrote of how crazed dancers of his region, across the Rhine from Strasbourg close to Freiburg im Breisgau, went to either of two chapels, one dedicated to St. John and the other to St. Vitus. There they danced furiously before the altar for three or more hours until they felt delivered from the madness.

"Results," said Grafenberg, "showed that in many cases they were right." The physician also noted that some dancers performed the ceremony every year. In the weeks beforehand they became "sad, shy, depressed, and anxious," their limbs hurt and twitched, and they claimed "they could never again be still or freed from the evil until they had danced before the chapel of the saints and thus driven out the madness."[192] They traveled to the shrine and once there they performed the dances they knew would plunge them into a state of temporary distraction.

Into the final years of the sixteenth century, this possession ritual flourished in a few locations in the Holy Roman Empire. In 1610 a jurist named Philipp Camerarius spoke of "a host of dancers not so long ago" who made sacrifices at a shrine of St. Vitus near Ravensburg, not far southeast of Strasbourg, and who "got well with his help" having "taken refuge here with their dancing."[193] Shortly after, the physician Gregor Horstius told of how "several people" every year "used to visit the chapel of St. Vitus near Geisling [near the town of Weissenstein]…in order there, in their delirium, to hop and dance day and night until they fell down in ecstasy. In this way they seem to have been cured to the extent that for a year following they felt little or nothing of the malady." At the same time the following year, they would again experience pain and cramps in their legs, tiredness, and "heaviness of the head" that only abated once they had danced manically at the St. Vitus shrine to the sound of musical instruments "played for their benefit."[194] Horstius wrote of one woman who had danced wildly every June 15 for thirty-two years. Another had danced alongside her annually for two decades.

These remarks draw our attention to a truly remarkable cultural phenomenon. In towns and villages of the western Holy Roman Empire, fear of the dancing curse had been harnessed and controlled. Those who felt vulnerable to being struck down by this saintly malediction could take part in rituals inspired by the belief that bouts of entranced dancing would protect them from worse forms of the saint's malice. These ceremonies satisfied the emotional cravings of the severely distressed as well as those marginalized by their communities. Dancing madly and deliriously for several hours was a means for them to channel and perhaps expel chronic feelings of anxiety. They rationalized their personal difficulties in terms of St. Vitus or St. John and then looked to an annual dancing pilgrimage as their only hope for an end to their troubles. Merely in anticipation of performing the healing dance they became agitated and their legs started to twitch and spasm. Then they headed for the shrine and took part in a classic possession ritual. But if some were helped by the catharsis of dance and the conviction that the saints would help, Gregor Horstius spoke of at least some poor women whose miseries lay much too deep to be danced away.

The possession states described by Grafenberg, Horstius, and Camerarius were very different from the involuntary trances to which the choreomaniacs were subjected. Those involved in the formal rituals of the St. Vitus cult actively desired the self-loss of trance and its duration was determined by their clear, unconscious expectations. The dancers of 1518, in contrast, entered terrifying trances with no pre-programmed sense of how long they should last. Yet there is clearly a link between the two sets of phenomena. Of the four possession cults connected to St. Vitus or St. John for which records survive, three occurred annually within a few day's ride to the east or south of Strasbourg. In all probability, the experience of the dancers of 1518 inspired the possession cults across the Rhine. The same might be true for the dancers of Muelebeek, for the towns of Flanders could easily be reached from Alsace by one of the boats plying these waters having carried salted fish from the Baltic and North Sea up to the cities of the Upper Rhineland. The town of Muelebeek was also, of course, a relatively short distance from Aachen, the center of the 1374 outbreak and even closer to Utrecht, the northernmost point reached by the same devastating epidemic.

There is a possibility, however, that the possession cults described by Grafenberg, Horstius, and Camerarius actually predated the curse of 1518.[195] In the remote communities east of the Black Forest, it could be that possession rituals involving wild dancing before images of St. Vitus went back almost as far as the saint's elevation to the status of holy helper. If so, talk of a wild dance that was both induced and cured by St. Vitus may have reached the people of Strasbourg in the years before the dancing plague hit. This too would help explain why they feared this saint and why performing sacred rituals before his shrine in Saverne rid so many of their morbid urge to dance.

The physician Grafenberg clearly perceived the connections between the dancing plague and the possession rituals in his own locality. But he also knew of a more direct parallel to the dancing cults of St. Vitus and St. John: the Italian tarantella.[196] For centuries, in scores of towns and villages in Sicily and the provinces of Apulia and Calabria on the southern mainland, men and women claiming to have been bitten by tarantulas called in players of the mandolin and tambourine to play for them so they could "dance out the poison." The musicians adjusted the tempo of their playing according to the "nature of the spider," for it was said that only the proper rhythm would induce a dance able to expel the venom. People danced the tarantella, frantic and languorous by turns, in a state of near-delirium, the rhythms of the music lulling them into the oblivion of trance. In reality, as Italian scientists discovered in the 1950s, tarantula bites have no psychotropic effects at all, but in a region where spiders are very common, it was easy, and presumably less stigmatizing, for the tarantellees to imagine that their psychological distress had a purely physical origin. The music of mandolin and tambourine then allowed the tarantellee to enter a trance during which they channeled and released their feelings of emotional unease. Like in the cases described by Plater, Grafenberg, Horstius, and Camerarius, prior to bouts of dancing that sometimes lasted for days, the tarantellees reported a mounting sense of anxiety. Those who performed the dance in farmhouses, barns, and squares from the Middle Ages right into the twentieth century appear to have shared this state of inner turmoil. Indeed, many tarantellees felt the need to dance the tarantella at around the same time each year, when their emotional conflicts clamored for a valid form of expression.

The tarantella ritual survived into the modern age, at least in remote villages in Apulia, but St. Vitus' Dance was fast disappearing as Grafenberg, Horstius, and Camerarius were writing. They were, essentially, writing its obituary. So, when in the later 1600s the English physician Thomas Sydenham wanted a term to describe a condition that involved the twitching and jerking of the limbs, he opted for "St. Vitus' Dance." No longer did the phrase conjure up images of wild dancers with glazed expressions moving with terrified, rapid abandon in streets and halls, of a convoy of frenzied men and women tightly wedged into wagons, or of scores of distracted people dancing around an altar. Unfamiliar with the old curse, Sydenham blithely appropriated its name. In the succeeding decades, St. Vitus' Dance became synonymous with "Sydenham's chorea," a condition involving spasms of the face, neck, body, arms, and legs which are probably the result of rheumatic fever. As time passed, it became ever harder to credit the descriptions of chroniclers like Specklin, Wencker, and Rem.

This prompts us to look more deeply into the reasons why the dancing plague vanished from the valleys of the Moselle and Rhine where it had preyed for so long on the anxious, unhappy, and alienated.

Chapter Eleven

DEATH OF A CURSE

In the summer of 1518 the inhabitants of Strasbourg experienced the last epidemic of crazed dancing that we know to have struck on European soil. Having haunted the peoples living along the Rhine and Moselle rivers for centuries, mass outbreaks of frenzied dancing stopped. Indeed, within just a few generations the idea of a deadly, dancing plague had become fantastic, even unbelievable. Yet in 1518, as in 1374, 1463, and on several other occasions, the dancing mania had been very real, frightening, and sometimes deadly.

The demise of St. Vitus' Dance is at one level easily explained. Afflictions that depend on the power of suggestion cannot survive without the beliefs that underpin them. Deprived of the supernaturalism on which it subsisted, choreomania was starved out of existence. We cannot really make sense of the disappearance of the dancing plague, however, without first understanding the reasons for the decline of the rich theology of the medieval and early modern worlds.

In Strasbourg, as elsewhere, the attacks on saint worship during the Reformation and the later Catholic Counter-Reformation were heavy blows. A Protestant rejection of saints' cults combined with a Papal crackdown on local variations in belief helped undercut the mysticism upon which the dancing plague had always thrived. Even so, Luther had been obsessed by the active influence of the Devil and his minions, while the resurgence of Catholicism in the 1500s saw pilgrimage roads and healing shrines once more thronged with the penitent and the pious sick. Moreover, it was during the same period that the Empire was convulsed by a long period of demonological paranoia resulting in the burning, drowning, and beheading of as many as 100,000 men and women accused of witchcraft. In fact, a clear trend toward a more sober skepticism is only perceptible after the middle decades of the seventeenth century. From then on, however, magical beliefs began to recede to the shadows, eventually becoming the preserve of rustics, the gullible, and the superstitious.[197]

The Scientific Revolution played a part in this profound shift in Western thought. A period stretching from roughly the 1540s till the early 1700s, it ushered in a firm conviction among natural philosophers that most phenomena could be reduced to simple cause and effect relationships that conformed to regular, natural laws. God had created the universe and then stepped back to allow his sublimely rational and ordered plan to unfold. The importance of mysterious forces, be they evil or good, was radically downsized. As Isaac Newton said: "Where natural causes are at hand, God uses them as instruments."[198] God had created the force of gravity, but he wasn't responsible for every meteor or falling apple.

Even more important were social and political crises. During the later 1600s many Europeans developed an aversion to religious enthusiasm after sectarian divisions, fueled in part by religious difference, had caused decades of brutal warfare and economic dislocation. Witnessing the effects of a century of carnage and persecution, many felt that extremes of piety had to be reined in. The same kind of religious enthusiasm was associated by many with the horrors of the witch-craze.[199] As the slaughter reached ever-greater heights of barbarity, virtually no one felt safe from being accused themselves or from the days of torture and probable execution that would follow. In this context, more and more people started to question the reality of witches and their magic. Thus, amid the ashes of thousands of pyres and hundreds of cities, towns, villages, and fields laid waste by warring bands of Catholics and Protestants, a restrained secularism came into vogue. Talk of witches, devils, demons, elves, miracles, God's flail, as well as saints' curses began slowly to decline.

The background of broader social and economic change was also relevant. An expansion of farming, the felling of pristine forest, an increase in urban living, and the development of new technologies meant that in a range of micro-environments nature seemed more predictable and susceptible to human control. Life started to seem less at the mercy of spiritual beings or celestial motions. It began to appear intelligible and rationally ordered. At the same time, the growth of market and later industrial capitalism, with their emphasis on the here and now, may have helped demystify people's views of the world they lived in.

In 1758, Cardinal Louis de Rohan, owner of a sumptuous new chateau in what was now the French town of Saverne, visited the St. Vitus shrine. There he found the collections of iron toads, walking sticks, and wax models. Appalled at what he saw as signs of shameful superstition, he banned anyone from leaving votive offerings.[200] Those desperate for the relief of illnesses where the cure lay beyond the power of medical science simply ignored the cardinal's ruling. But the tide had turned. No longer was there a holy hermit to greet them as they reached the summit. In fact, after a long period of decline, by the early nineteenth century the chapels were derelict and being used as cattle sheds. Thus, as religious enthusiasm waned, as elite culture spurned supernaturalism, and as science came to occupy a more privileged place in Western culture, the veneration of St. Vitus and the fear of his curse both died slow deaths.

Cardinal Rohan's skepticism also highlights a fast-expanding division, far less familiar to the world of the early sixteenth-century, between the cultures of the elites and the common folk. In 1518, as in 1374 and 1463, civil and ecclesiastical officials had been willing to accept the idea that the dance was a divine or diabolical curse. In doing so they had lent credence to the people's paranoia. Within little more than a century of the Strasbourg epidemic, uneducated notions of the supernatural realm were more likely to elicit scorn and disgust from the higher social ranks. If many of the inhabitants of Europe went on believing in spirits, ghosts, witches, and divine intercessions, they tended to do so without the approval of the ruling classes. The elites had come to practice their faith with less emotional intensity than before. Even if pilgrimages continued and the residents of Echternach still held their annual dancing procession, declining numbers of people felt that every sickness, injury, meteor, or "monstrous" birth had its origin in the divine.[201] The dancing plague was losing its cultural niche.

Yet bizarre events like the dancing epidemic of 1518 tend to live long in the popular imagination, even if they are romanticized, distorted, and shorn of their original context. While the idea of a real penitential dance that could prove fatal disappeared in the 1600s, some memory of it may have survived in the form of folklore. During the early nineteenth century, as Napoleon's forces mustered along the German borders, the brothers Grimm were busy harvesting folk tales, legends, songs, and rhymes that they believed would reveal the very soul, or Volkspoesie, that united all the German peoples.[202] They drew their stories from old books and manuscripts; from well-educated friends who vividly recalled the tales told by nursemaids, governesses, and servants; from an old soldier (in exchange for secondhand clothes); and from a tailor's wife. Among their crop of stories was that of Snow White that, in its unbowdlerised form, climaxes with the wicked stepmother being forced to wear red-hot iron slippers and "dance until she fell down dead." It is at least possible that this gruesome detail contains a memory of one of the more salient moments of the 1518 dancing plague. Similarly, Hans Christian Andersen's *The Red Shoes* tells of a young girl whose vanity is punished by her having to wear red shoes that make her dance in ceaseless agony. Only by having an executioner chop off her feet is she able to stop. The source of Andersen's tale is unclear. It's presumably related in some way to his father's career as a cobbler, but it too might have drawn on elements of popular culture infused with stories of the dancing mania of 1518 and the red shoes handed out to those afflicted by the St. Vitus curse. It would be fitting if these stories did contain echoes of the past, as St. Vitus' Dance was to a large degree the result of the creative imagination.

We should not, however, forget the real victims of the dancing curse. Compared to smallpox, plague, dysentery, measles, and tuberculosis, the death toll from these epidemics was of course minute. The scale of fatalities also pales against the numbers of peasants slaughtered in Saverne in 1525 and in the countless other battles, skirmishes, sieges, and raids of this turbulent and bloody period. We're talking here of at most hundreds of deaths due to dancing rather than the hundreds of thousands claimed by warfare or the plague. Yet many more people had been afflicted by the curse than had actually died: from the eleventh to the sixteenth centuries, somewhere in the order of several thousand had probably succumbed to a terrifying compulsion to dance. They experienced excruciating anguish in the weeks before and still greater horrors during their days of wild entrancement.

Almost too strange for the modern mind to comprehend, the medieval and early modern epidemics of dancing are relatively unknown today. Indeed, so profoundly had European society changed by the late twentieth century that some medical writers felt entitled to ignore virtually everything that the Strasbourg chroniclers had recorded, claiming instead that the choreomaniacs suffered from a severe form of frontal lobe epilepsy. In a relatively sober and secular present, it is of course hard to believe that our predecessors could have danced themselves to death. Yet chroniclers like Rem, Wencker, and Specklin described real events with considerable accuracy. They knew what epilepsy looked like and the witnesses upon whom they relied saw something quite different. Moreover, those twentieth-century writers who asserted that the choreomaniacs were simply epileptic could have found, had they looked, a striking modern case of dancing mania, an outbreak that was recorded by a coolly secular Scottish physician.

This last recorded case of an epidemic of uncontrollable dancing began in Madagascar in February 1863.[203] It was dubbed *imanènjana* by the local population and, as one Dr. Davidson later reported, it quickly engulfed thousands of people and continued for several weeks. In the streets of the capital and in solitary hamlets, people danced for hours or days at a time to the sound of drums and other instruments. Some recovered, having danced themselves into a stupor of exhaustion, but many of them later returned to the dance, especially if they again heard the beat of a drum. The similarities with earlier outbreaks of choreomania are striking. The physician told of how the eyes of the dancers were "wild," their "whole countenance assumed an indescribable abstracted expression, as if their attention was completely taken off what was going on around them," and they made few sounds other than frequent deep sighs. Evidently they were in a state of trance. For this reason, Dr. Davidson had no difficulty in distinguishing the genuinely afflicted: none could imitate their crazed expressions or their incredible power of endurance. As in the Strasbourg case of 1518, in Madagascar the lower classes were most susceptible. More importantly, the epidemic was said to have been triggered by "a general spirit of dissatisfaction and superstitious unrest." The people of the island worshipped numerous deities who were believed to be active in the world, for good or ill. They believed implicitly, as did the people of the Holy Roman Empire in 1518, in sorcery, witchcraft, the magical powers of idols and icons, and the need to propitiate supernatural beings. Madagascar's choreomaniacs seem to have believed themselves possessed by the spirit of the late Queen Ranavalona; hence many left offerings of sugar canes at a sacred stone where rulers of

Madagascar had been crowned or around tombs where they could communicate with the dead. Reminiscent of the 1374 dancing plague, the Madagascan dancers also had strong aversions, in this case to hats, which embodied a fierce dislike of the Europeans who were seen to be meddling in their country, and to pigs, traditionally considered unclean and proscribed by the late queen.

It was clear to Dr. Davidson that the wild dancers of 1863 were reacting to intolerable levels of social, economic, and spiritual despair. Just two years before, Queen Ranavalona had passed away after a rule of appalling barbarity. Much of the nation was now in a state of chronic anxiety as it awaited invasion by either the British or French, their sense of foreboding intensified by news that the new king had secretly converted to Christianity. To Dr. Davidson it was also apparent that religious (or what he and his contemporaries called "idolatrous") beliefs had translated the people's anguish into the form of a crazed dance. We don't exactly know how "superstitious unrest," as Dr. Davidson called it, was converted into compulsive dancing. It's probably relevant, however, that missionaries of the nineteenth century told of tribal ceremonies in which some communities in Madagascar danced in breathless worship. In addition, there is a long tradition of trance rituals being performed across the island.[204] These possession rituals, during which entranced mediums "receive" the spirits of the dead, often take place at tombs like those to which Dr. Davidson tells us the afflicted dancers traveled in 1863. Most of these spirits are believed to be those of deceased royalty, so the burial places of kings, queens, and their relations have a special significance. We can safely assume, then, that thousands of Madagascans danced because they believed their souls to have been displaced by royal spirits who were exacting a terrible revenge; in particular, they considered themselves possessed by the spirit of Queen Ranavalona who was despairing in her afterlife of the pro-European policies being implemented by her son and heir. This is why the dancers headed for tombs and other places that had symbolic associations with royalty and there left their offerings. Like the choreomaniacs of 1518, they supplicated the angry spirits.

Davidson's report is extremely important since it so fully corroborates accounts of Strasbourg in 1518. These two sets of dancers, separated by vast swathes of time, space, and cultural practice, nonetheless thought and behaved in essentially the same fashion. In both cases misery was closely coupled with a belief in the wrath of vengeful spirits; the dancers were reduced to a trance state in which they could not control their movements; music played for their benefit intensified their trance states and often triggered relapses in those who seemed to have recovered; the lower social ranks were disproportionately affected; and perhaps most significantly, victims and onlookers imagined the dance to be both a supernatural punishment and its own remedy. Davidson witnessed the same powerful interplay of fear, suffering, and religion observed by Brant, the members of the XXI, and the Imlin'sche chronicler more than four centuries before. And Davidson knew that it was a hysterical reaction because the Christian neighbors of the afflicted, who ate the same food, drank the same water, and breathed the same air, virtually never succumbed to the plague. As Davidson explained, the Christians did not share the same beliefs as their "heathen countrymen" nor did they have the same fear and hatred of Western influence. Hence they were largely immune. So when Davidson subsequently read of the European dancing plagues in a book by a German scholar named J.F. Hecker, he had no difficulty in seeing that the dancers of 1863, 1518, and 1374 were all victims of "some popular idea or superstition, at once so *firmly* believed as to lay hold of the heart of the people, and so *generally* as to afford scope for the operation of pathological sympathy."

For Davidson in Madagascar, as for Brant and the Imlin'sche chronicler in Strasbourg, the dancing mania was weird and horrible. It violated rules of proper conduct even if it was quite compatible with both the florid theologies of medieval Christianity and the spirit worship of the people of Madagascar. Yet Davidson hinted at an important truth: that the dancing manias could not have happened had it not been for the potential strangeness inherent in all of us. In the deepest distress, our minds have the capacity to assume states and to trigger actions that are shocking and bizarre but that also make sense in the context of our irrational fears and beliefs. The behavior of the dancers of 1374, 1518, and 1863 may have been impulsive, yet it was also choreographed by the expectations and practices of their worlds. In what ways, then, are the cerebral pathways responsible for the dancing mania still operative today? Making sense of choreomania leads us to consider some of our stranger psychological capabilities.

THE MIND
INCARNATE

Chapter Twelve

CHARCOT'S ERROR

The dancing plagues seem thoroughly at home amid the catastrophes of premodern Europe, fitting additions to that dour tapestry of war, plague, and religious violence. Yet the events of 1518 were not as singular as they may at first seem. Epidemics of dancing were responses to a combination of misery, suggestion, and belief. In this crucial sense, they were extreme manifestations of cerebral processes that in other forms are still very much with us. Brains under severe strain have always produced sensations and behaviors which, although beyond volitional control, reflect the ideas and expectations of sufferers and the societies in which they live. Some of these disturbances are dramatic, such as spontaneous trance, compulsive movements, mutism, anesthesias, and paralysis, while others are more subtle, for example, persistent fatigue and psychogenic pain. Just like the dancing epidemics, they highlight the remarkable fact that even when we lose control, we often do so in culturally prescribed ways. This concluding chapter looks at what we know of the baffling mental processes that underpinned outbreaks of choreomania and related psychic phenomena today.

The nature of spontaneous trance is the key to understanding not only the dancing plagues, but also innumerable other cases of flamboyantly wild behavior. While it's among the most puzzling of mental states, trance is neither rare nor idiosyncratic. Indeed, anthropologists calculate that more than 90 percent of modern cultures have rituals in which entrancement routinely takes place, while psychologists have identified at least eighteen altered states, in addition to the more mundane processes of sleeping and dreaming. A few of these can be learned, like possession trance or deep meditation; several are deemed pathological, for example fugue states, somnambulism, and the "splitting" of consciousness associated with dissociative identity disorder (DID), while some are just a little strange, like the transient feeling many people experience of somehow not being associated with their physical body. These states all have in common a fragmentation or sidelining of normal consciousness, what modern psychiatrists typically refer to as "dissociation."[205]

The disruption of consciousness in the form of

trance entails a number of cognitive changes. These include an impairment of critical analysis, reality checking, and rational thought; a breakdown in the normal perception of space and time; an increase in suggestibility to internal or external stimuli; a related tendency to confuse fantastic ideas and visions for reality; and a heightened threshold for tolerating pain. The dancing mania of 1518 conforms closely to these criteria for trance. A distorted sense of time and a relative insensitivity to pain allowed the choreomaniacs to dance near-continuously for days or even weeks. Meanwhile, they also became easy prey to imagined fears of St. Vitus and his curse while lacking the conscious awareness necessary to challenge their supernaturalist beliefs. Their minds were, in effect, commandeered by ideas that would have been strongly resisted by the executive control centers of the brain while in full waking consciousness.

There are several ways of inducing this kind of psychic disintegration.[206] One is through extreme sensory bombardment. Repetitive singing, clapping, drumming, circular dancing, and head movements, as well as rapid changes from light to dark and powerful olfactory stimulation such as the burning of incense, may serve to overwhelm normal consciousness. Trance can also be achieved through becoming very highly focused on just one or two stimuli, disrupting the normal, broken flow of consciousness; this certainly accords with the yogic meditation practice of concentrating on a single thought or image and the use of a metronome or swinging watch to induce hypnosis. There are also physiological correlations to the tendency to dissociate. In particular, malnutrition may play a role. Diets low in minerals can interfere with the production of the neurotransmitter serotonin, potentially leading to abnormal psychological states.[207] Since low-status women in many cultures have had poorer diets than their husbands, this may help explain why they are usually overrepresented among those suffering from spontaneous trances.

In addition, extreme psychological distress can induce trance. Hence those living in austere convents, strict boarding schools, or harshly run factories have been among the most prone to experience dissociative states. The role of stress is quite apparent in the advent of the dancing plague in Strasbourg. The same is true for the outbreaks of 1374, which occurred just months after one of the worst floods in modern European history struck the valleys of the Rhine and Moselle; chronicles tell of the waters of the Rhine rising thirty-four feet, of flood waters pouring over the walls of Cologne, of homes and market places submerged and of decomposing horses bobbing along watery streets.[208] It is unlikely to be a coincidence that the

1374 dancing plagues of Holland, the western fringe of Germany and northeastern France spread in just those areas most severely affected by this devastating flood: their crops ruined and animals killed and their belief in divine protection badly shaken, some would have been easily unhinged. But if most choreomaniacs were the victims of grinding worry built up over years or months, sudden, acute dread can also precipitate a trance state. Freefall skydivers are, for instance, at risk of entering trance, and there are numerous cases from the First World War of soldiers who, dug from under the debris hurled up by exploding shells, wore the distant, disconnected look of the deeply entranced.[209]

At the level of neurology, trance is complex and ill-understood. There is, though, some rough-and-ready evidence that suggests the involvement of unusual dynamics between the left and right hemispheres of the brain. Drawing on the findings of MRI and PET scans, some neuroscientists have argued that certain kinds of stimuli may so wholly occupy the attention of the left hemisphere, the side most involved in analytical and logical thought, that the right hemisphere, with its higher capacities for imagination, fantasy, and creativity, is able to gain preeminence; thus the entranced often lose their sense of reality, believing to be true even their wildest thoughts and imaginings. This is only one of several neurological models of trance induction, though it may provide further explanation for why the choreomaniacs danced for so incredibly long. Since repetitive motion intensifies trance, it might be that the dancing itself kept their left hemispheres from regaining control.

Any attempt to explain the onset of trance must also take into account the often awesome power of suggestion. An altered state, like spontaneous trance, is far more likely to be produced in an individual who expects it to happen. Such is apparent from the case of Strasbourg in 1518 when Frau Troffea's dance turned epidemic once onlookers had become convinced that a wrathful St. Vitus was stalking their city. Another striking example of the contagiousness of trance involves the Ursuline nuns of the southern French town of Loudun. In 1643, Jeanne des Anges, Mother Superior of a local nunnery, fell in love with a local priest, Urbain Grandier, who seems barely to have been aware of her existence. Troubled by illicit dreams about the priest, Jeanne des Anges subjected herself to flagellation and other severe forms of penance. Nothing helped alleviate her guilt. Deeply distressed, she eventually slipped into a trance. While writhing, shaking, and speaking in strange and devilish tongues, she claimed to have been bewitched by Father Grandier. The event might have attracted little attention beyond the town had it not been for the fact that over the following days several more nuns, their minds rendered suggestible by their Mother Superior's "bewitchment," also became entranced and behaved in the same outrageous fashion. For months they periodically returned to the trance state. With few local friends, and having unwisely made powerful enemies, Father Grandier was burnt at the stake on the strength of the nuns' accusations.[210]

Modern-day Malaysia and Singapore provide further examples of the role of suggestibility in the triggering of spontaneous trance. In both countries, factory workers are often recruited from among rural migrants—men and women who share traditional beliefs about spirits and possession. When a worker, apparently unable to cope with the harsh authoritarianism of the factory regime, plunges into a trance, others perceive the action of evil spirits and, in consequence, some of them reproduce the identical symptoms. Such outbreaks are usually brought to an end with religious ceremonies and, often, the sacrificing of a goat to appease the gods.[211]

Probably the best evidence of human suggestibility and its role in trance induction comes from studies of possession cults. Indeed, so suggestible a species are we that most human groups have, at one time or another, been able to cultivate the ability to experience trance. Thousands of well-documented possession rituals demonstrate how minds can be prepared, by learning or passive exposure, to shift into different states of consciousness. In fact, spontaneous trance is a regular occurrence in many communities. Among the Samburu pastoral nomads of northern Kenya, young men routinely enter trances in stressful moments, such as when they are outdanced by rival groups. Reflecting on similar examples, the American anthropologist Erika Bourguignon speaks of an "environment of belief," the set of accepted ideas about the spirit world that members of communities absorb, thus preparing them later to achieve the "possession state."[212] Watching possession rituals, hearing about them, and anticipating one day joining in places the mind in a state of readiness to switch into an alternative mode of consciousness in which reality is distorted and strange fantasies seem concretely real. Some cultures are highly systematic in preparing for a few members, usually shamans, to undergo ritual trance. In the Brazilian Candomblé cult, novices are schooled in the art of shamanic trance by adepts, spending weeks together in a state of semi-trance before being formally initiated as adepts themselves.[213] Not that it's necessary to be formally trained. The dancers of Strasbourg and the nuns of Loudun likewise occupied an "environment of belief" that took seriously the perceived threat of divine curse, posses-sion, and bewitchment. They didn't intend to become entranced, but they too were rendered suggestible by a shared set of supernaturalist beliefs.

Modern possession rituals also reveal how powerfully the participant's thoughts and actions are guided by their culture's beliefs and expectations; in fact, some experts argue that trance is nothing more than a state of extreme suggestibility. Take, for instance, the tarantellees of southern Italy and Sicily who danced themselves into oblivion. Convinced that their misery was due to the effects of spider venom, they sought to dance their depression away and did so in a prescribed form. Many of them assumed the likeness of a spider by bending backward until they were supporting themselves on palms and heels. Similarly, the participants in Haitian Vodou rituals adopt the roles of specific deities drawn from a pantheon of gods with varying personalities. Female mediums in Madagascar likewise take on the distinct personas of the spirits believed to inhabit them, be they kind, impish, greedy, or vindictive.[214] The Kung of the Kalahari have two trance rituals, each with different rules. In the "Giraffe Dance," those entering trance (or *kia*) approach the sick and, by laying their hands on them, "pull" out sickness and hurl it back to the spirit realm. They also claim to perceive hidden sicknesses, to see spirits at the edge of the camp, and travel to the land of the gods.[215] In contrast, participants in the Kung's women-only "Drum Dance" are not expected to heal. Instead they are supposed to "shiver and shake while standing in place." Proper conduct in both ceremonies is strictly defined and those who fail to observe the conventions can be forbidden from undergoing *kia*, a very powerful sanction within Kung communities.

There are, obviously, fewer rules in spontaneous trances than in possession rituals, but cultural associations are still clearly mobilized. The "possessed" Ursulines of Loudun exemplify this fact, for although they had apparently never been schooled in possession, they acted in just the manner expected of the bewitched or the demonically possessed: writhing, foaming, convulsing, dancing, laughing, speaking in strange tongues, and making obscene gestures and propositions. These were shocking but at the same time entirely stereotypical performances based on deep-seated beliefs about Satan's cunning and depravity. The same explanation may well apply to the female choreomaniacs of 1374 who, if several Dutch and imperial chroniclers are to be believed, bared their breasts and freely offered up their virginity to bystanders. It's presumably because the dancers of 1518 believed themselves to have been cursed from Heaven, rather than Hell, that there are no reports of them indulging in lascivious behavior. Similarly, the hallucinatory visions of medieval and early modern mystics like Joan of Arc conformed to narrow expectations of what a genuinely divine experience entailed. Not only was there a prescribed formula for the bona fide mystical experience, but even at an unconscious level mystics seem to have appreciated that they risked charges of heresy if their testimony conflicted with Church doctrine.

The long tradition of ecstatic religion provides us with many more parallels to choreomania, since the more extravagant of spiritual movements have also been fueled by the combination of psychological distress, suggestion, and cultural conditioning. Many religions, moreover, have cultivated trance. As the Bible-scholar Ronald Knox explained, entering an altered state in which one feels a deep sense of peace or speaks in strange tongues provides an indication of a divine presence, a deeply reassuring sensation among those subject to savage persecution for their beliefs.[216] The early Quakers, for instance, practitioners of a proscribed religion, were said in the 1650s to hold meetings during which they were "strangely wrought upon in their bodies, and brought to fall, foam at the mouth, roar, and swell in their bellies." The entranced participants were left with an exquisite sense of having been touched by God. Likewise, the early Shakers of New York sang and danced until they entered trances. With extraordinary stamina, they then leapt over and over again high into the air. Sometimes, one witness recorded, they would "clap hands and leap so as to strike the joyce [joists] above their heads."[217]

Perhaps the most striking case of ecstatic religion comes from the American South where, in the 1790s, the "Great Awakening" began. Enormous prayer meetings were held, often lasting four or more days, during which preachers harangued thousands with the folly of their sins and spoke in lurid detail of the horrors of Hell. Worked into frenzies of fear and guilt, worshippers succumbed to the "falling sickness": they would loudly shriek, fall to the ground, lose consciousness, and writhe around, often hallucinating. Many also experienced violent jerking, resulting in bizarre contortions; others got down on all fours and barked like dogs; and some danced for hours in a manner strongly reminiscent of the choreomaniacs. As the historian George Rosen pointed out, the participants in the Great Awakening typically lived in hostile environments, exposed to high levels of sickness and regular attack by native tribes. Just like many of the Quakers and Shakers, they were drawn by distress to mind-altering worship.[218]

Pentecostal churches maintain the ecstatic traditions of the Great Awakening. In the trance state, the Pentecostal worshipper's sense of reality is suspended as they are imbued with a powerful feeling of being infused by the Holy Spirit. Once the individual's ability to draw rational inferences has been weakened or put on hold, they experience feelings of ecstasy, speak in tongues, or fall to the floor, in accordance with the particular conventions of their congregation. The majority of recruits to Pentecostalism have always been the poor, the lonely, and the oppressed, the experience of religious trance providing reassurance to those with feelings of isolation, unhappiness, or despair.[219]

Outside of Pentecostal churches, deliberately induced trances are rarely witnessed in the secular West. Secularism has undermined the "environment of belief" that impelled many of our ancestors to enter altered states when confronted with severe levels of stress. This is not to say, however, that trance is the only state of mind in which people articulate their anguish in a bizarre fashion. Most epidemics of odd behavior involve distortions to the thought processes of people who are entirely conscious. This is well illustrated by the periodic outbreaks of koro in Southeast Asia and China.[220] In times of political or economic uncertainty and in a region where masculinity is strongly associated with the male genitalia, thousands of men come to believe that their penises are shrinking into their bodies and that death will ensue if they become fully retracted. The victims of this terrifying fear arrive at medical clinics clutching their penises in a desperate attempt to keep them from receding any further. In many cases, the terror does not subside until exorcism ceremonies have been held to expel the "supernatural fox maidens" believed to be causing the potentially fatal genital retraction.

Perhaps more reminiscent of the dancing plague is the laughing epidemic that in 1963 engulfed the region to the west of Lake Tanganyika in Tanzania.[221] Several girls at a mission school began spontaneously to laugh and cry by turns. Soon 95 out of 159 pupils had succumbed and the school had to be closed down. But sending the girls back to their villages simply spread the epidemic to other children and, in a fraught post-colonial context, some adults were affected as well. The physicians who charted the epidemic's rise and fall recorded several hundred individual cases, with victims on average laughing for an entire week, their suffering interspersed with short periods of remission. No biological hypotheses as to its cause stood up to the scrutiny of blood tests and microscopic analysis. What really clinched the case was that the sickness did not affect any adults who were "literate" or "relatively sophisticated." In other words, those lacking in strong supernaturalist beliefs were immune. The investigators explicitly concluded that epidemic laughter was analogous to the dancing plagues of medieval Europe.

The cases of koro and the Tanzanian laughter epidemic demonstrate that suggestibility to terrifying beliefs increases in times of distress whether we're conscious or not. Nor is the secular West invulnerable to hysterical fears. In fact, some are virtually endemic. American and to some extent European cultures remain awash with paranoid delusions of alien abduction and flying saucers. Psychiatry is itself partly to blame for other epidemics of suggestion. As the historian Elaine Showalter points out, in recent decades some psychiatrists, with exaggerated ideas as to the prevalence of child sexual abuse, have helped implant baseless memories of incest in many patients' minds.[222]

Medically more significant than mass hysteria is a condition in which patients present with odd movements and gaits, paralyses, tics, mutisms, blindness, anesthesias, and mysterious pains that have no identifiable organic cause. Blood tests, EEGs, MRIs, and PET scans reveal zero trace of infection, lesions, or structural damage. Doctors do, however, elicit histories of depression, trauma, or abuse. Cases like these are typically labeled as "conversion disorder," based on the idea that a patient's psychological pain has manifested itself in the form of disturbances to voluntary motor or sensory function. Opinions vary as to the prevalence of conversion disorder. One study found that about 35 percent of patients referred to neurology clinics presented with disorders with no apparent medical basis. Between 1 and 2 percent of these patients exhibited voluntary motor or sensory dysfunction that seemed to be psychological in origin.[223]

In recent years neuroscientists have made significant advances in showing that conversion disorder is a physical reality. One study involved a woman with a long history of depression and trauma who presented with a paralyzed left leg. A battery of tests revealed no evidence of organic damage that could explain her paralysis. For the experimenters she was an ideal test subject since they could compare her brain activity when she tried to move her right leg against what happened when she strove to move her left leg. She could provide, in short, her own experimental control. The results of PET scans were striking. As expected, areas of the brain involved in motor function were activated when the patient prepared to move her right leg. More importantly, activity in the same regions of the brain was triggered when she was getting ready to move her paralyzed left leg as well. The patient, this suggested, was not feigning: she had every intention of moving. But when it actually came to moving her left leg, the woman's brain reacted in a very distinctive way compared to when she successfully moved her right. Parts of the brain known to be involved in the integration of emotion and action were strongly activated. These appear to have inhibited her instruction for the left leg to move. Her will was being countermanded.[224]

Perhaps the most remarkable feature of conversion disorder is that its expression appears to be subtly shaped by prevailing ideas and expectations. In this basic sense it shares an important characteristic with medieval choreomania. Ironically, some of the best evidence that psychological distress can be converted into somatic forms was produced by a man who spent his career arguing the opposite. He was called Jean-Martin Charcot. Dubbed "the Napoleon of the neuroses," during the 1880s Charcot became one of the most famous doctors in the world.[225] Before reverential gatherings at the Salpêtrière asylum in Paris, he would hypnotize his female "hysterics" so as to trigger fits during which they would spasm, hallucinate, and convulse, become mute or lose sensation, while their limbs became twisted and contorted, and some collapsed to the floor with their spines, arms, and heads curved backward toward their feet in what was called the *arc de cercle*. No mere showman, Charcot was the preeminent student of "hysteria," a term covering a vast range of motor and sensory disturbances that he said originated in tainted heredity and damaged nerves. Charcot did concede that hysteria often first appeared after psychological trauma, but he insisted that the form the attacks took was determined by cast-iron physiological laws. Hysteria, said Charcot, follows a path inscribed in the nervous system itself. He even identified four phases of the attack: they began with an epileptic-like fit, moved onto bodily contortions, then a spell of impassioned poses, and terminated in various ways, often involving delusions and hallucinations.

In one sense Charcot was right. His patients' hysterical attacks often did pass through the four stages he identified. Yet he had been royally fooled. Many of his patients convulsed and spasmed not according to inviolable natural laws, but because these were highly suggestible individuals who had been housed alongside patients with severe epilepsy; as a result their neurotic fits had assumed the pattern of epileptic seizures.[226] Moreover, once Charcot had outlined his four-stage theory of hysteria, his neurotic patients were quick to conform to it, becoming ever more adept at satisfying his expectations. Eager for Charcot's warm approval, they involuntarily acted out the movements that most gratified the famous medical professor. Few of these women were conscious that they were gulling poor Charcot. Even in a hypnotic state they acted out what their minds knew him to be seeking.

It does not seem to have troubled Charcot, in his drive to discover laws of hysteria every bit as fundamental as Newton's laws of planetary motion, that the four-stage hysterical attacks he described hardly occurred outside the Salpêtrière asylum. One of his juniors, the Strasbourg-educated Jules-Joseph Dejerine, wondered if his boss hadn't created a carnival of suggestion.[227] Charcot was not to be lightly crossed, but Dejerine was right: there are no iron laws of hysteria.

Charcot's reputation didn't long survive his death, but his contribution to the history of psychiatry was still profound. Quite inadvertently, he had provided a clear demonstration of the suggestibility of the human unconscious. His work showed just how outlandish an individual's symptoms can be when acute anxiety is coupled with beliefs already located in the mind or implanted from outside. After the 1880s, psychiatrists and neurologists were far more willing to see hysterical symptoms as originating in psychological distress. Often they went too far. Sigmund Freud, for instance, returned to Vienna having studied with Charcot convinced that all manner of pains, paralyses, and spasms were neurotic. Setting up as a private "nerve doctor," he proceeded to misdiagnose many of his patients, like a Mr. Stransky who experienced pain in his arm as a result of cancer, not the hysteria diagnosed by Freud.[228]

In spite of the untestability of many of their ideas, Freud's followers rose to prominence in psychiatric circles, especially in post-Second World War America. Bread and butter for generations of psychoanalysts was explaining the spasms, paralyses, altered states, pains, and low moods of their clients in terms of unresolved childhood sexual conflicts. In the last twenty years the Freudian Empire in America has largely disintegrated. But for all their faults and overconfidence, the Freudians did a valuable service by insisting, against Charcot and his admirers, that physical symptoms can be the result of ideas stored in the unconscious.

Among the most striking cases of the power of the mind in mediating the expression of trauma was one documented by the English shellshock doctor, Lewis Yealland, in 1916. A private who had experienced all the hell of the trenches had collapsed, unable to speak. Yealland believed that such patients got well only if they were convinced that they were suffering from treatable organic conditions: he understood the power of suggestion. So, he employed electrotherapy, a technique which soldiers could be persuaded was a straightforward medical treatment. Like hundreds of other mute patients, this private was electrocuted in the neck and throat. When, at last, he started to mutter, his left arm began to tremor. Yealland gave it a bolt of electricity. Then the tremor switched to the right arm, "then [to] the left leg, and finally [to] the right leg." There are few better illustrations of the psychological rather than physiological nature of conversion disorder than Yealland's chasing symptoms around this poor man's body, electrodes at the ready. Unfortunately, many of Yealland's "cures" were short-lived; his methods were better contrived to remove obvious symptoms (albeit temporarily) than to treat the underlying psychological causes.[229]

Even if hysterical symptoms like those experienced by Dr. Yealland's patient look as if they are independent of place and time, they too can be culturally conditioned. The historian Edward Shorter argues that hysterical symptoms have waxed and waned over the centuries in line with changing modes of thought and expectation. What he calls the "symptom pool" varies through time and with it the variety of conversion symptoms. As we have already seen, during the Middle Ages and early modern period men and women who had crossed a threshold of emotional endurance often broke down in ways that conformed to stereotypes of witchcraft, mysticism, or demonic possession. Several historians and psychiatrists have argued that, with the rise of secularism, emotional breakdowns began to emulate medical fashions rather than religious tropes. Writhing, foaming, and issuing denunciations in strange voices became a less and less legitimate way to fall apart. Those who behaved in this manner were more liable to be stigmatized as insane rather than bewitched. As a result, new forms of hysteria came to the fore. Hysterical paralysis, says Shorter, had been rare before the 1800s but became almost pandemic when doctors started to speak of the dangers of nerve damage and spinal inflammation. Likewise, when European physicians started to discuss the phenomenon of somnambulism, they triggered a wave of sleepwalking.[230]

The relationship between conversion symptoms and cultural context is sharply revealed by the experience of the traumatized soldiery of the First World War. As leading psychiatrists recognized, not everyone expressed the horror of attritional conflict in the same manner. Battlefront doctors were convinced that when the nerves of officers and infantrymen snapped, they did so in very different ways. The lower ranks trembled, twitched, found themselves rendered dumb, mute, and partially blind, they lost control of their limbs, or walked in the strangest of manners. In other words, they behaved rather like the female hysterics made famous by Charcot and Freud. Frontline British officers, in contrast, were said to suffer more from night-terrors, irrepressible anxiety, and mood swings, the assorted symptoms that are now collected under the label "post traumatic stress disorder." Developing histrionic symptoms may just not have been an option for an officer class schooled in the absolute necessity for self-composure and emotional restraint.[231]

Perhaps the most salient development in the modern history of hysteria has been a more general shift away from dramatic motor symptoms during the twentieth century. Writing in 1982, the French psychoanalyst Jacques Lacan mused: "Where are the hysterics of former times, those magnificent women, the Anna Os and Emmy von Ns?"[232] Mutisms, convulsions, paralyses, altered states, and sensory deficits due to anxiety seem to be less common today than in any time over recorded history. This trend was perceptible even during the First World War, as military hospitals were deluged with men suffering from an almost certainly nervous condition dubbed "Disordered Action of the Heart" that involved chest pains, giddiness, and palpitations.[233] During the Second World War, there were even fewer cases of the flamboyant hysterias of the Victorian era. Today, severe stress is far more likely to be expressed in a form psychiatrists call "somatoform disorder," involving psychogenic pain (often headaches and stomach or bowel discomfort), fatigue, dizziness, or a general sense of malaise.[234] Research in rural India provides strong evidence for this movement toward the less overt somatoform disorder. In two well-studied Indian villages, rates of conversion disorder fell significantly between 1972 and 1987. Far more people now complain of pain and fatigue than motor paralysis or sensory loss. This shift has been attributed to a general increase in the mental health of women due to improved access to schools and, just as importantly, education having reduced "public credulity."[235]

Psychiatrists may have identified a reason why

conversion symptoms often seem to be tailored to the wider cultural context. They argue that conversion is an unconscious means of eliciting sympathy, or what is called "secondary gain." The argument goes that because psychological disorders have always been highly stigmatizing, the unconscious mind does what it can to camouflage the emotional nature of the individual's problems and expresses the kinds of symptom most likely to call forth pity and assistance. The concept of "secondary gain" is used by medical anthropologist Arthur Kleinman to account for why depressed patients in China seem to complain of aches, pains, and fatigue more often than they do of the low mood or anxiety most frequently reported in the West.[236] Mental illnesses are so stigmatized in China that (Kleinman says) psychological distress is more safely expressed in the idiom of physical disease. The depressed are at least then spared the shame of mental illness. By implication, these conversion symptoms are proportionately less common in the Western world because there temporary bouts of depression and anxiety tend to be less damaging to one's reputation. As most authors emphasize, secondary gain does not imply that sufferers are duplicitous. Their pain is real, often excruciating, and deserving of whatever help it manages to elicit.

The claim that conversion disorder is a means of obtaining sympathy is plausible but hard to test. All

we can safely say is that the symptom pool for conversive symptoms does seem to have changed broadly in
keeping with the decline in magical beliefs and, subsequently, shifts in disease theory and medical diagnoses.
On the other hand, we know that some cases of conversion disorder have very little to do with a culturally
mandated symptom pool. Sometimes the expression
of anxiety is clearly related to the specific nature of
the individual's traumas or fears. For example, there
are reports of Victorian ladies with anesthesias (*i.e.*
insensitivity to touch) stretching from the tops of their
gloves to the bottoms of their blouse sleeves. Their
symptoms make no physiological sense but probably
reflected an agonizing level of personal modesty. The
horrors of war have produced similar reactions. In 1940
a soldier arrived home from Dunkirk with a paralyzed
hand.[237] It emerged that he had used the same hand to
hold the gun with which he killed his brother whom
he found dying from a stomach wound on the retreat.
Combat psychiatrists also wrote of soldiers troubled by
stomach pains in the same area where they had bayo-
neted enemy combatants or snipers with blindness in
the eye with which they had aimed their rifles. Once
again, conversion symptoms were the manifestation of
ideas rather than being the expressions of an underlying
organic disorder.

Discussing possession trance, ecstatic religion,

and conversion disorder may seem to have taken us a long way from the dancing plagues of Europe and Madagascar. In fact, there are several important parallels. For a start, choreomania and conversion disorder both highlight the absurdity of such statements as "it's only stress." People of the more secular West typically break down in a fairly restrained manner. However terrible the pain, in comparison to the Middle Ages or even the Victorian age the individual's behavior is usually reserved. And yet the histories of spontaneous trance and conversion disorder tell us that we have within us the capability to respond to life's vicissitudes in much more dramatic fashion, be it in the form of violent writhing, frantic dancing, hysterical mutism, paralysis, or compulsive laughing. Psychological trauma is capable of profoundly altering mental function, severing voluntary control over our bodies, and plunging us into dissociative states in which our imaginations and fantasies can take command of our actions. Evidently, for all the clichés of problems being "only in the mind," the effects of trauma and distress are anything but trivial or superficial. Indeed, despite modern psychiatry's fast-expanding battery of medications, the prognosis for those suffering from conversion disorders sadly remains poor.

Choreomania and conversion disorder also remind us that few disorders of the mind can be classified with the same precision as typical organic conditions. Measles, typhoid, cholera, smallpox, and dysentery are all expressed in ways that have virtually nothing to do with the culture of times and places. Standards of nutrition, housing, sanitation, and medical knowledge will of course affect their prevalence and severity, but the connection between underlying physiology and symptomology is close and relatively predictable. The same is not true for the vast swathe of symptoms assembled under diagnoses like dissociation, conversion, or somatoform disorder. The forms these take depend fundamentally on beliefs and if we are to make sense of them then we first need to understand the cultural worldviews of those who succumb.

Epidemics of wild dancing seem utterly mystifying when looked at from the point of view of secular modernity, when most of us struggle to imagine what it felt like to believe that God, the Devil, and their underlings exercised tight control over the minutest affairs of humankind. Generations of writers offered explanations for the events of the summer of 1518 which drew upon their own prior experiences, imaginations, and beliefs. What virtually no one did prior to such modern historians as Alfred Martin, George Rosen, and, especially, H.C. Erik Midelfort was attempt to recover the prior experiences, imaginations, and beliefs of the wretched people who felt themselves to be in the grip of saintly wrath. Only having taken this step can we appreciate that choreomania offers us an object lesson in how cultural conventions can determine the manner in which pathological anxiety is expressed. Just as importantly, it offers us a striking case study in the extreme suggestibility of our species, especially when under conditions of severe psychological stress.

Maybe it's time to write the epitaph of the dancing plague. Yet that might be a little premature. An innocent witness of one of the illegal "raves" that took place in the English countryside during the 1980s or of today's thriving all-night clubbing scene might well be tempted to draw comparisons with the wild dancing of 1374, 1463, and 1518. There are few contemporary spectacles quite as exotic as thousands of young men and women crowded into darkened clubs dancing throughout the night with the most avid intensity, their minds consumed by rhythm and rapid beats, seldom pausing to drink or rest. There are, of course, profound differences between clubbing and choreomania. The clubbing phenomenon is fueled by recreational drugs, like MDMA (i.e., ecstasy), which combined with the activity of dancing seem to enhance the individual's sense of kinship with fellow clubbers.[238] Moreover, the moments of euphoria dancers experience are more akin to the ecstasies of Pentecostal worship than the psychological agonies of the dancing mania. Yet there is also a striking resemblance. Their consciousness of fatigue lessened by drugs, clubbers have a capacity to dance for extraordinary, occasionally fatal, lengths of time. Dancing through the night, largely heedless of bodily exhaustion, they reproduce at least some of the bizarreness of the dancing plague. In this limited sense we might see clubbing as the chemical equivalent of the original St. Vitus' Dance. Certainly, anyone unconvinced that an altered state of mind could have impelled thousands of people in 1518 to dance for days on end, will have their doubts dispelled by witnessing the modern-day clubbing phenomenon. Paracelsus, who saw choreomania as a just punishment for dancers' levity, would have had an apoplexy.

ENDNOTES

1. This account of Frau Troffea's dance is based largely on
    Paracelsus' description in his 1531 work, *Opus Paramirum*;
    only he provides a name for the first person to succumb to
    the dance frenzy. See Theophrastus Paracelsus, *Volumen
    Paramirum und Opus Paramirum* (Jena: E. Diederichs,
    1904). A translation of this and other contemporary
    accounts can be found in Eugène Louis Backman, *Religious
    Dances in the Christian Church and in Popular Medicine*,
    translated by E. Classen (London: Allen & Unwin,
    1952), pp. 314–15. See also George Rosen, *Madness in
    Society: Chapters in the Historical Sociology of Mental Illness*
    (London: Routledge & K. Paul, 1968), which contains a
    detailed discussion of the dancing manias; the English
    language version of Justus Friedrich Carl Hecker, *The
    Black Death and the Dancing Mania*, translated by B.G.
    Babington (London: Cassell, 1894); and the highly inci-
    sive analysis in H.C. Erik Midelfort, *A History of Madness*

in Sixteenth-Century Germany (Stanford, Calif.: Stanford University Press, 1999). There are useful discussions of the dancing mania of 1518 (and previous outbreaks) in Alfred Martin, "Geschichte der Tanzkrankheit in Deutschland," *Zeitschrift des Vereins fur Volkskunde*, vol. 24 (1914), pp. 113–34, pp. 225–39; Sibylle Gross, *Hans Wydyz: sein Œuvre und die oberrheinische Bildschnitzkunst* (Hildesheim: Olms, 1997); Robert E. Bartholomew, *Little Green Men, Meowing Nuns, and Head-Hunting Panics: A Study of Mass Psychogenic Illness and Social Delusion* (Jefferson, N.C.: McFarland, 2001); Jean F. Russell, "Dancing Mania," in *Festschrift for Kenneth Fitzpatrick Russell* (Carlton, Vic.: University of Melbourne, 1978), pp. 161–96; Madeleine Braekman, "La Dansomanie de 1374: Heresie ou Maladie?" *Revue du Nord*, vol. 63, no. 249 (1981), pp. 339–55; L.J. Donaldson, J. Cavanagh, and J. Rankin, "The Dancing Plague: A Public Health Conundrum," *Public Health*, vol. 111, no. 4 (1997), pp. 201–4; Hellmuth Liebscher, *Ein Kartographischer Beitrag zur Geschichte der Tanzwut* (dissertation, Leipzig, 1931); and E.C. Wicke, *Versuch einer Monographie des grossen Veitstanzes und der unwillkürlichen Muskelbewegung* (Leipzig, 1814). Several works, including Hecker's classic *The Black Death and The Dancing Mania*, misdate the Strasbourg epidemic. Martin's "Geschichte der Tanzkrankheit" showed conclusively, as do the Strasbourg chronicles themselves, that it took place in 1518 rather than in 1418.

2. Paracelsus' report, translated in Backman, *Religious Dances*, p. 314.

3. Kleinlawel, *Strassburgische Chronik, der kurtze Beschreibung von Ankunfft, Erbaw, und Erweiterung der Statt Strassburg, wie auch vom Leben, Regierung, und Absterben der Bischoffen daselbsten* (Strassburg, 1625), pp. 130–1. Translation from Midelfort, *Madness*, p. 48.

4. Much of this book is based upon the following published chronicles, which were either written at the time or, more typically, compiled later from contemporary documents found in the city archives: *Bulletin de la Société pour la Conservation des Monuments Historiques d'Alsace* (Strasbourg, 1898), contains *Les Collectanées de Daniel Specklin*. "Les Annales de Sébastián Brant," gathered together by Jacques II Wencker in the late 1700s from extant documents (most of them since lost or destroyed) can be found in Abbé L. Dacheux (ed.) *Bulletin de la Société pour la Conservation des Monuments Historiques d'Alsace* (Strasbourg, 1892) and *Bulletin de la Société pour la Conservation des Monuments Historiques d'Alsace* (Strasbourg, 1899); the 1892 volume also contains the "Chronique de Jean Wencker" and the "Supplément a la Chronique de Wencker." The Duntzenheim chronicle is contained in the *Bulletin de la Société pour la Conservation des Monuments Historiques d'Alsace* (Strasbourg, 1897), p. 12. See also Karl Stenzel's *Die Straßburger Chronik*, p. 74; Rudolf Reuß, *Strassburg im sechzehnten Jahrhundert (1500–1591); Auszug aus der*

Imlin'schen Familienchronik (Colmar, 1875), pp. 24–5; Wilhelm Rem, *Chronika newer Geschichten. Bearbeitet von Friedrich Roth. Chroniken deutscher Städte 25* (Leipzig, 1896); Jacob von Königshoven, *Älteste teutsche so wol allgemeine als insonderheit elsassische und straßburgische Chronicke* (Strassburg: Städel, 1698); Karl Stenzel, *Die Straßburger Chronik des Elsassischen Humanisten Hieronymus Gebwiler* (Berlin, 1926), p. 74.

5. From Parlacelsus' *Von den Krankheiten, so den Menschen der Vernunft berauben* (Strassburg, 1576). For translations see *Four Treatises of Theophrastus von Hohenheim, Called Paracelsus*; translated from the original German, with introductory essays, by C. Lilian Temkin, George Rosen, Gregory Zilboorg, and Henry E. Sigerist (Baltimore: Johns Hopkins Press, 1941), pp. 157–61 and pp. 180–3.

6. Philip Ball, *The Devil's Doctor: Paracelsus and the World of Renaissance Magic and Science* (New York: Farrar, Straus and Giroux, 2006), p. 45.

7. Ernst E. Metzner, *Zur frühesten Geschichte der europäischen Balladendichtung. Der Tanz in Kölbigk: Legendarische Nachrichten, gesellschaftlicher Hintergrund, historische Voraussetzungen* (Frankfurt: Athenäum 1972). For the subsequent outbreaks in Wales, Erfurt, Maastricht, the massive epidemic of 1374, and the smaller incident of 1463, see Backman, *Religious Dances* (this is by far the most detailed treatment in English); Martin, "Geschichte der Tanzkrankheit"; Hecker, *The Dancing Mania*; Rosen,

Madness in Society; Midelfort, *Madness*; and Russell, "Dancing Mania." For more information on the 1463 outbreak see Paul Hoffmann and Peter Dohms, *Die Mirakelbuecher des Klosters Eberhardsklausen* (Düsseldorf: Droste Verlag GMBH, 1988), pp. 110–11. There is a description of the 1374 epidemic in Johannes Trithemius, *Chronik des Klosters Sponheim* (Bad Kreuznach: Jean-Winckler-Str. 4, Selbstverl, 1969).

8. Backman, *Religious Dances*, pp. 216–30, speculates that the victims of the dance were pilgrims from Bohemia. If this is true, there is no evidence that they came intending to dance, nor that ritualized dancing was typical worshipful behavior in their homeland.

9. See Liebscher, *Ein Kartographischer*, as well as Midelfort, *Madness*, p. 33. I have found no convincing evidence for Liebscher's claim that the dancing epidemic spread to England.

10. See Backman, *Religious Dances*, pp. 303–21 and Mary Kilbourne Matossian, *Poisons of the Past: Molds, Epidemics, and History* (New Haven: Yale University Press, 1989), pp. 56–7, for attempts to implicate ergot (though Matossian misdates the Strasbourg epidemic to 1418). Mervyn J. Eadie's "Convulsive Ergotism: Epidemics of the Serotonin Syndrome," *The Lancet* (Neurology), Vol. 2 (July 2003), pp. 429–34, considers the case for ergotism. I am grateful to Mervyn Eadie, Professor of Neurology at the University of Queensland, for his assistance in

eliminating ergot poisoning as a likely cause for the dancing mania. See also Donaldson, Cavanagh, and Rankin, "The Dancing Plague," pp. 201–4 and G. Berger, *Ergot and Ergotism* (London: Gurney and Jackson, 1931).

11. Several fine examples can be seen in the Alsatian Museum in Strasbourg. It is not clear when the link was made in this region between ergotism and poisoned grain.

12. See Rosen, *Madness in Society*, chapter 7 and Hecker, *The Dancing Mania*.

13. See Amy Greenfield, *A Perfect Red: Empire, Espionage, and the Quest for the Colour of Desire* (Black Swan, 2006), p. 27.

14. For an introduction to the late medieval view of man and nature see Owen Barfield, *Saving the Appearances; A Study in Idolatry* (London: Faber and Faber, 1957).

15. See Victor E. Thoren, *The Lord of Uraniborg: A Biography of Tycho Brahe* (Cambridge University Press, 1990), p. 213.

16. For the Ensisheim meteor see Christiane Andersson, "Polemical Prints in Reformation Nuremberg," in Jeffrey Chipps Smith (ed.) *New Perspectives on the Art of Renaissance Nuremberg: Five Essays* (Austin: Archer M. Huntington Art Gallery, College of Fine Arts, University of Texas at Austin, 1985), pp. 41–62, specifically pp. 42–4. For Brant's theology and cosmology also see Larry A. Silver, "Nature and Nature's God: Immanence in the Landscape Cosmos of Albrecht Altdorfer," *Art Bulletin* 91 (1999),

pp. 194–214. A brief biography of Brant is contained in Charles Schmidt, *Histoire littéraire de l'Alsace à la fin du XVe et au commencement du XVIe siècle* (Nieuwkoop, B. de Graaf, 1966).

17. For late medieval millenarianism see Norman Cohn, *The Pursuit of the Millennium* (London: Secker & Warburg, 1957), especially p. 21.

18. Schmidt, *Histoire littéraire*, p. 338. Schmidt also describes Geiler's tenderheartedness.

19. Miriam U. Chrisman, *Strasbourg and the Reform: A Study in the Process of Change* (New Haven: Yale University Press, 1967), p. 69. The claim that the bodies of children had been found buried near cloisters was an old one. For the generally lamentable state of the Strasbourg church and the moral failings of the clergy see: Frances Rapp, *Réformes et Réformation a Strasbourg: Eglise et Société dans le Diocese de Strasbourg* (1450–1525) (Strasbourg: Association des Publications près les Universties de Strasbourg, 1974); Chrisman, *Strasbourg and the Reform*, especially chapters 4 and 5; Lorna Jane Abray, *The People's Reformation: Magistrates, Clergy, and Commons in Strasbourg, 1500–1598* (Ithaca: Cornell University Press, 1985); Thomas A. Brady, *Ruling Class, Regime and Reformation at Strasbourg, 1520–1555* (Leiden: Brill, 1978); Amy Leonard, *Nails in the Wall: Catholic Nuns in Reformation Germany* (Chicago: University of Chicago Press, 2005); Elsie Anne McKee, *Katharina Schütz Zell* (Leiden: Brill, 1999); William S.

Stafford, *Domesticating the Clergy: The Inception of the Reformation in Strasbourg, 1522–1524* (Missoula, Mont.: Scholars Press for the American Academy of Religion, 1976); and Thomas A. Brady, "Rites of Autonomy, Rites of Dependence: South German Civic Culture in the Age of Renaissance and Reformation," in Steven Ozment (ed.), *Religion and Culture in the Renaissance and Reformation* (Kirksville, Mo.: Sixteenth Century Journal Publishers, 1989), pp. 9–24.

20. For the often fruitless attempts at reform in monasteries and convents see Rapp, *Réformes*, book 2, chapter 1. Also useful is Leonard, *Nails in the Wall*, chapters 2 and 3, especially pp. 24–9.

21. For attitudes toward clerical vice among the laity see Francis Rapp, chapter 4 of Georges Livet and Francis Rapp, eds., *Histoire de Strasbourg des Origins à Nos Jours Livet* (Strasbourg: Editions Privat, 1987) and Rapp, *Réformes*, especially books 3 and 4; and Stafford, *Domesticating the Clergy*, early chapters.

22. Chrisman, *Strasbourg and the Reform*, pp. 3–13; Francois-Joseph Fuchs, "Les foires et la rayonnement economique de la ville en Europe," book 5 of Georges Livet and Francis Rapp, *Histoire de Strasbourg* (Editions Privat, 1987), pp. 259–306; Freddy Thiriet, "Sur les Relations Commerciales entre Strasbourg et L'Italie du Nord à la Fin du Moyen Age," *Revue D'Alsace*, vol. 100 (1961, 121–8); Georges Lévy-Mertz, "Le Commerce Strasbourgeois au

XVe Siècle D'apres les Règlements de la Douane," *Revue D'Alsace*, vol. 97 (1958), 91–114; Tom Scott, *Regional Identity and Economic Change: The Upper Rhine, 1450–1600* (New York: Oxford University Press, 1997); Jean Rott, "Artisanat et mouvements sociaux a Strasbourg autour de 1525," in *Artisans et Ouvriers d'Alsace* (Strasbourg, 1965); and Brady, *Ruling Class*, various chapters.

23. See A. C. Hanauer, *Etudes Economiques sur l'Alsace Ancienne et Moderne* (Paris 1876–8), vol. 1, p. 39, p. 93; and Rapp, *Réformes*, pp. 436–7.

24. See H. J. Cohn, "Anticlericalism in the German Peasants' War," *Past & Present*, vol. 83, no. 1 (1979), pp. 3–31.

25. See Cohn, *Pursuit of the Millennium*, pp. 113–4. Just as unforgivable was the practice of the Strasbourg Chapters of buying up parishes, paying the curates a measly wage, and then skimming off the remainder in profit. See the attacks on clerical corruption in Gerald Strauss, *Manifestations of Discontent in Germany on the Eve of the Reformation* (Bloomington: Indiana University Press, 1971).

26. For social tensions see Brady, *Ruling Class*.

27. Rapp, *Réformes*, p. 406; Adolf Laube, "Precursors of the Peasant War: *Bundshuh* and *Armer Konrad*—Movements at the Eve of Reformation," in Janos Bak (ed.), *The German Peasant War of 1525* (London: Frank Cass, 1976), pp. 49–53. For the *Bundschuh* movements also see: Albert E. Rosenkranz, *Der Bundschuh, die Erhebungen des*

südwestdeutschen Bauernstandes in den Jahren 1493–1517 (Heidelberg: C. Winter, 1927); Thomas Adam, *Joß Fritz—das Verborgene Feuer der Revolution* (Ubstadt-Weiher: Verlag Regionalkultur, 2002); Peter Blickle and Thomas Adam (eds), *Bundschuh: Untergrombach 1502, das unruhige Reich und die Revolutionierbarkeit Europas* (Stuttgart : Steiner, 2004); Tom Scott, *Freiburg and the Breisgau: Town-Country Relations in the Age of Reformation and Peasants' War* (Oxford: Clarendon Press, 1986); and Lawrence G. Duggan, *Bishop and Chapter: The Governance of the Bishopric of Speyer to 1552* (New Brunswick: Rutgers University Press, 1978).

28. Rapp, *Réformes*, pp. 442–9.

29. Roland Oberlé, *La vie quotidienne en Alsace au temps de la renaissance* (Strasbourg: Oberlin, 1983), chapter 5 and p. 121. For carnivals see Peter Burke, *Popular Culture in Early Modern Europe* (London: Temple Smith, 1978); Emmanuel Le Roy Ladurie, *Carnival: A People's Uprising at Romans, 1579–1580*, translated from the French by Mary Feeney (London: Scholar Press, 1980); Barbara Ehrenreich, *Dancing in the Streets: A History of Collective Joy* (New York: Metropolitan Books, 2006), p. 92.

30. Sebastian Brant, *The Ship of Fools*; translated into rhyming couplets, with introduction and commentary, by Edwin H. Zeydel (New York: Columbia University Press, 1944).

31. See Paul Adam, *Charité et Assistance en Alsace au Moyen Age* (Strasbourg: Libraire Istra Strasbourg, 1982), p. 207;

Oberlé, *La vie quotidienne*, p. 94; Jacques Heran (ed.), *Histoire de la Médicine à Strasbourg* (Strasbourg: La Nuee Bleue, 1997), pp. 82–4.

32. Quoted in Jon Arrizabalaga, John Henderson, and Roger French (eds.), *The Great Pox: The French Disease in Renaissance Europe* (New Haven: Yale University Press, 1997), p. 26.

33. See Heran, *Histoire de la Médicine*, p. 84.

34. See Sander L. Gilman, "AIDS and Syphilis: The Iconography of Disease," *October*, vol. 43 (1987), pp. 87–107, p. 92.

35. Silver, "Nature and Nature's God," pp. 208–9.

36. Oberlé, *La Vie Quotidienne*, p. 91.

37. See Marie Antony-Schmitt, *Le Culte de saint Sébastien en Alsace: médecine populaire et saints guérisseurs: essai de sociologie religieuse* (Strasbourg: Librairie Istra, 1977); and Hieronymus Brunschwig, *Pestbuch* (Strassburg: Johann Reinhard Grüninger, 1500). Consistent with Samuel Cohn's arguments about the relatively high status of medical explanations by this period, Brunschwig also listed a series of physical remedies. See Samuel K. Cohn, Jr., "The Black Death: End of a Paradigm," *American Historical Review*, vol. 37, no. 3 (2002), pp. 703–38. There is still considerable debate as to whether or not the Black Death really was caused by Yersinia pestis and spread by the fleas on the common black rat.

38. Francis Rapp, "L'Église et les Pauvres à la fin du Moyen

Age: l'Exemple de Geiler de Kaiserberg," *Revue D'Histoire de L'Église de France*, vol. 52 (1966), pp. 39–46.

39. Miriam U. Chrisman, *Lay Culture, Learned Culture: Books and Social Change in Strasbourg, 1480–1599* (New Haven: Yale University Press, 1982), p. 79.

40. For butchers and meat provision, as well as economic life in general, in Strasbourg see Scott, *Regional Identity*, chapter 7.

41. Cohn, *Pursuit of the Millennium*, pp. 115–20.

42. See Rapp, *Réformes*, p. 487.

43. Scott, *Freiburg and the Breisgau*, p. 177. See also "Supplément a la Chronique de Wencker" (1892), p. 202.

44. Quoted in Jean Lebeau & Jean-Marie Valentin, *L'Alsace au Siècle de la Réforme: Textes et Documents* (Presses Universitaires de Nancy, 1985), pp. 90–1.

45. See Rapp, *Réformes*, pp. 157–9.

46. Ibid., pp. 244–8.

47. Ibid., p. 349. For a handsome fee some clergy agreed to pursue the laity's debtors in the ecclesiastical courts. Many a peasant indebted to a layman found himself homeless and excommunicated as a result. See Rapp, *Réformes*, p. 349. See also William S. Stafford, *Domesticating the Clergy: The Inception of the Reformation in Strasbourg, 1522–1524* (Missoula, Mont.: Scholars Press for the American Academy of Religion, 1976), p. 29 and Cohn, "German Peasants' War."

48. Quoted in Brady, "Rites of autonomy," p. 13.

49. Specklin, *Les Collectanées*, p. 480.

50. Quoted in Brady, "Rites of autonomy, rites of dependence," p. 18.

51. See Specklin, *Les Collectanées*, p. 481. See also Chrisman, *Strasbourg and the Reform*, p. 70. Not that von Hohenstein was unduly upset. He seemed perfectly content to keep as his personal vicar a monk who cohabited with the concubine who had mothered his brood of children.

52. Rapp, *Réformes*, p. 349.

53. See Rossell H. Robbins, *The Encyclopedia of Witchcraft and Demonology* (New York: Bonanza Books, 1981), p. 218. See also Joseph L. Koerner, *The Moment of Self-Portraiture in German Renaissance Art* (Chicago: University of Chicago Press, 1993).

54. Chrisman, *Lay Culture*, p. 79.

55. See C. Arnold Snyder and Linda A. Huebert Hecht, eds., "Margarethe Prüss of Strasbourg," *Profiles of Anabaptist Women: Sixteenth-Century Reforming Pioneers* (Waterloo, Ont.: Wilfrid Laurier University Press, 1996), p. 264. Hanauer, *Etudes Economiques*, p. 40 and p. 94.

56. "Annales de Sébastian Brant" (1892), p. 231.

57. For the 1511 *Bundschuh* see Rapp, *Réformes*, p. 407; Rosenkranz, *Der Bundschuh*; Adam, *Joß Fritz*; Scott, *Freiburg and the Breisgau*.

58. See Brady, "Rites of Autonomy."

59. "Annales de Sébastian Brant" (1892), p. 234.

60. Quoted in Chrisman, *Strasbourg and the Reform*, p. 14.

61. See Valentin Groebner, *Liquid Assets, Dangerous Gifts: Presents and Politics at the End of the Middle Ages* (Philadelphia: University of Pennsylvania Press, 2002), p. 47.

62. Rudolf Reuß, *Strassburg im sechzehnten Jahrhundert (1500–1591); Auszug aus der Imlin'schen Familienchronik* (Colmar, 1875), pp. 24–5.

63. Dean P. Bell, *Sacred Communities: Jewish and Christian Identities in Fifteenth-Century Germany* (Leiden: Brill Academic Publishers, 2001), p. 21.

64. "Annales de Sébastian Brant" (1892), p. 234.

65. Reuß, *Auszug aus der Imlin'schen*, pp. 24–5. See also Charles Boersch, *Essai sur la mortalité à Strasbourg: Thèse présentée et publiquement soutenue à la Faculté de médecine de Strasbourg* (France: s.n., 1836), pp. 119–20.

66. "Annales de Sébastian Brant" (1892), p. 234.

67. Specklin, *Les Collectanées*, pp. 305–6. See also Francis Rapp, *L'Église et la vie religieuse en Occident à la fin du Moyen Age* (Paris: Presses Universitaires de France, 1971), pp. 143–5; and Elsie Anne McKee, *Katharina Schütz Zell* (Leiden: Brill, 1999), p. 21.

68. See Robert Schwoebel, *The Shadow of the Crescent: The Renaissance Image of the Turk, 1453-1517* (New York: St. Martin's Press, 1967), esp. chapter 5.

69. "Supplément a la Chronique de Wencker" (1892), p. 202. See also Reuss, *Imlin'schen Familienchronik*, pp. 24–5; Rapp, *Réformes*, pp. 438–40; Boersch, *Essai sur la Mortalité*, p. 119; and Hanauer, *Etudes Economiques*, p. 40.

70. Quoted in Lorna Jane Abray, *The People's Reformation: Magistrates, Clergy, and Commons in Strasbourg, 1500–1598* (Ithaca: Cornell University Press, 1985), pp. 50–1.

71. Hanauer, *Etudes Economiques*, p. 40.

72. "Supplément a la Chronique de Wencker" (1892), p. 202.

73. See Rapp, *Réformes*, pp. 440–1, p. 438, and book 5, chapter 2; Boersch, *Essai sur la Mortalité*, pp. 119–20.

74. See "Annales de Sébastian Brant" (1892), p. 236. For Strasbourg's hospitals see Paul Adam, *Charité et Assistance en Alsace au Moyen Age* (Strasbourg: Libraire Istra Strasbourg, 1982); Heran, *Histoire de la Médicine*; and Oberlé, *La vie quotidienne*, chapter 4. For economic conditions in 1517 also see Backman, *Religious Dances*, p. 238.

75. See Antony-Schmitt, *Le Culte de saint Sébastien*, p. 63.

76. For depopulation in the region due to plague see Tom Scott, ed., *The Peasantries of Europe: From the Fourteenth to the Eighteenth Centuries* (London: Longman, 1998), p. 114. See also Wilhelm Abel, *Geschichte der deutschen Landwirtschaft vom frühen Mittelalter bis zum 19. Jahrhundert, Deutsche Agrargeschichte*, vol. 2 (Stuttgart, 1962), p. 103.

77. For leprosy in Strasbourg see Adam, *Charité et Assistanc*; Heran, *Histoire de la Médicine*; and Otto Winckelmann, *Das fürsorgewesen der stadt Strassburg vor und nach der reformation bis zum ausgang des sechzehnten jahrhunderts; ein beitrag zur deutschen kultur—und wirtschaftsgeschicht* (Leipzig, 1922), pp. 30–3. For leprosy in 1517 see

Backman, *Religious Dances*, p. 238. Such was the shortfall in paying for the care of the lepers that in 1518 and 1519 additional donations were necessary; see Winckelmann, *Das fürsorgewesen*, p. 32.

78. Specklin, *Les Collectanées*, p. 488.

79. Rapp, *Le Diocèse de Strasbourg*, p. 72.

80. Gebwiler, *Die Strassburger Chronik*, pp. 74–5. See also Winckelmann, *Das fürsorgewesen*, p. 43, p. 54; and Adam, *Charité et Assistance*, p. 16.

81. See Rapp, *Réformes*, and Brady, "Rites of Autonomy," for the rising tide of anticlericalism.

82. H.C. Erik Midelfort also identifies July 14 as a likely start date, though it may have been a day or two either side.

83. *Bulletin de la Société pour la Conservation des Monuments Historiques d'Alsace* (Strasbourg, 1897), p. 12.

84. Translated by Backman, *Religious Dances*, pp. 314–5.

85. Henricus Institoris and Jacobus Sprengler, *Malleus Maleficarum* (1487); edited and translated by Christopher Mackay (Cambridge University Press, 2006), pp. 112–22.

86. Cited in Midelfort, *Madness*, p. 71.

87. Reuss, *Imlin'schen Familienchronik*, p. 25.

88. Winckelmann, *Das fürsorgewesen*, pp. 73–4.

89. See Adam, *Charité et Assistance*, p. 93 and p. 103.

90. "Annales de Sébastian Brant" (1892), pp. 237–8 and Adam, *Charité et Assistance*, p. 104.

91. See McKee, *Katharina Schütz Zell*, p. 22; and William Henry Klaustermeyer, *The Role of Matthew and Catherine*

Zell in the Strassburg Reformation (unpublished PhD thesis, Stanford University, 1965), p. 41. For the decline in charitable donations to most religious orders in Strasbourg, see Rapp, *Réformes*, pp. 397–404.

92. Martin Eels, *Martin Bucer* (New Haven: Yale University Press, 1931), p. 21.

93. See Klaustermeyer, *Role of Matthew and Catherine Zell*, p. 40 and Eels, *Martin Bucer*, p. 21.

94. See Margaret W. Labarge, *Women in Medieval Life* (London: Penguin, 2001).

95. Backman, *Religious Dances*, pp. 232–3; Martin, "Geschichte der Tanzkrankheit," cited on p. 116; and Salomon Vögelin, *Geschichte der Wasserkirche in Zürich* (Zürich, 1848).

96. See Backman, *Religious Dances*, p. 243.

97. For a summary of biological factors involved in trance-induction, including malnutrition, see Tara L. AvRuskin, "Neurophysiology and the Curative Possession Trance: The Chinese Case," *Medical Anthropology Quarterly*, vol. 2, no. 3 (1988), pp. 286–302. See also Charles T. Tart, ed. *Altered States of Consciousness* (San Francisco: Harper, 1990). For more information on the remarkable Plater family, see Emmanuel Le Roy Ladurie, *The Beggar and the Professor: A Sixteenth-Century Family Saga*, translated by Arthur Goldhammer (Chicago: University of Chicago Press, 1997).

98. See the translations in Backman, *Religious Dances*, chapter 13, and Midelfort, *Madness*, pp. 32–3.

99. See Otto Brunfels, *Onomasikon, seu lexicon medicinae simplicis* (Strasbourg: Joannes Schottus, 1543). Entry on "Corybantes." See also Claire Biquard, "Le mal de saint Vit (ou saint Guy)," *Bulletin du Centre d'étude d'histoire de la medicine*, no. 39 (2002), pp. 33–50.

100. Frances Rust, *Dance in Society: An Analysis of the Relationship between the Social Dance and Society in England from the Middle Ages to the Present Day* (London: Routledge & K. Paul, 1969), p. 45.

101. Quoted in Peter Burke, *Popular Culture in Early Modern Europe* (New York: Harper & Row, 1978), p. 217. For the power of dance see William H. McNeill's excellent *Keeping Together in Time: Dance and Drill in Human History* (Cambridge, Mass.: Harvard University Press, 1995) and Ehrenreich, *Dancing in the Streets.*

102. Quoted in Rosemary Horrox, *The Black Death* (Manchester: Manchester University Press, 1994), p. 107.

103. Quoted in Backman, *Religious Dances*, chapter 13 and pp. 289–90. See also Hecker, *Dancing Mania.*

104. For the St. Vitus legend see Biquard, "Le mal de saint Vit" and Backman, *Religious Dances*, pp. 264–7.

105. See A. Adam, *Sankt Veit bei Zabern Oder der Hohle Stein* (Zabern, 1879).

106. Ibid.

107. See Backman, *Religious Dances*, p. 195, p. 203, and p. 211.

108. Quoted in Midelfort, *Madness*, pp. 32–3. See also Paul Hoffmann and Peter Dohms, *Die Mirakelbuecher des*

Klosters Eberhardsklausen (Düsseldorf: Droste Verlag GMBH, 1988), pp. 110–11.

109. Johannes Trithemius, *Chronik des Klosters Sponheim* (Bad Kreuznach, 1969), p. 123.

110. See Egon Schmitz-Cliever & Herta Schmitz-Cliever, "Zur Darstellung des Heiltanzes in der Malerei im 1500," *Medizinhistorisches Journal*, vol. 10 (1975), pp. 307–16.

111. "Annales de Sébatien Brant" (1892), p. 236.

112. Martin, "Geschichte der Tanzkrankheit," pp. 120–21. See also Midelfort, *Madness*, p. 37.

113. See Backman, *Religious Dances*, pp. 116–26. See also Paul Krack, "Relics of Dancing Mania: The Dancing Procession of Echternach," *Neurology*, vol. 53 (1999), pp. 2169–72.

114. Backman, *Religious Dances*, p. 265 and p. 109; Voltaire, *A Philosophical Dictionary* (London: John and Henry L. Hunt, 1824), p. 19.

115. See Philip Ball, *The Devil's Doctor: Paracelsus and the World of Renaissance Magic and Science* (New York: Farrar, Straus and Giroux, 2006).

116. Specklin, *Les Collectanées*, p. 300.

117. For extreme penitential acts see Walter Vandereycken, *From Fasting Saints to Anorexic Girls: The History of Self Starvation* (London: Athlone Press, 1994).

118. See Backman, *Religious Dances*, chapter 13.

119. Gebwiler, *Die Strassburger Chronik*, p. 74. Translated in Midelfort, *Madness*, p. 34.

120. Quoted in William Tydeman, *The Medieval European Stage, 500–1550* (Cambridge: University of Cambridge Press, 2001), p. 657.

121. Backman, *Religious Dances*, p. 191.

122. See Gilbert Rouget, *Music and Trance: A Theory of the Relations between Music and Possession* (Chicago: University of Chicago Press, 1985), chapter 1.

123. "Annales de Sébastian Brant" (1892), p. 239.

124. For Strasbourg politics and government see Thomas A. Brady, *Ruling Class, Regime, and Reformation at Strasbourg, 1520–1555* (Leiden: Brill, 1978) and Thomas A. Brady, *Protestant Politics: Jacob Sturm (1489–1553) and the German Reformation* (Atlantic Highlands, N.J.: Humanities Press, 1995).

125. "Annales de Sébastián Brant" (1899), p. 252.

126. Quoted in Backman, *Religious Dances*, p. 203 and p. 209.

127. Johann Gutenberg appears to have perfected his printing technology while living in Strasbourg in 1440.

128. "Annales de Sébastián Brant" (1892), p. 237. See also Heran, *Histoire de la Médicine*, p. 70.

129. See Lynn Thorndike, *A History of Magic and Experimental Medicine* (New York: Columbia University Press, 1941), pp. 431–4 and Heran, *Histoire de la Médicine*, p. 53.

130. Quoted in Backman, *Religious Dances*, p. 238.

131. "Annales de Sébastián Brant" (1899), p. 252.

132. Quoted in Dale B. Martin, *The Corinthian Body* (New Haven: Yale University Press, 1995), pp. 19–20. See

also Elizabeth C. Evans, "Galen the Physician as Physiognomist," *Transactions and Proceedings of the American Philological Association*, vol. 76 (1945), pp. 287–98.

133. See Antony-Schmitt, *Le Culte de Saint Sébastien*, pp. 67–8.

134. "Annales de Sébastián Brant" (1899), p. 252.

135. John Ray, *Observations Topographical, Moral, & Physiological Made in a Journey through Part of the Low-Countries, Germany, Italy, and France* (London, 1673), p. 411.

136. For this comment and an exposition of what a strictly orthodox Galenist might have felt about trying to dance the madness away see Nicholas Culpeper, *Galen's Art of Physick...Translated into English, and Largely Commented on: Together with Convenient Medicines for all Particular Distempers of the Parts, a Description of the Complexions, Their Conditions, and What Diet and Exercise Is Fittest for Them* (London: Peter Cole..., 1652), p. 63. See also Charles Burnett, "'Spiritual medicine': music and healing in Islam and its influence in Western medicine," in Penelope Gouk, ed. *Musical Healing in Cultural Contexts* (Brookfield, USA: Ashgate, 2000), p. 89. See also Alessandro Arcangeli, "Dance and Health: The Renaissance Physicians' View," *Dance Research*, vol. 18, no. 1 (2000), pp. 3–30.

137. Ambroise Paré, *Oeuvres Complètes*; edited by J.F. Malgaigne (Paris: J.B. Baillière, 1840–1841), p. 52.

138. See Backman, *Religious Dances*, pp. 232–3.

139. "Annales de Sébastián Brant" (1892), p. 148. On the

relative standing of the guilds see Chrisman, *Lay Culture*, p. 24 and pp. 307–8; and John D. Derksen, *From Radicals to Survivors: Strasbourg's Religious Nonconformists over Two Generations* (De Graaf Publishers, 2002), p. 22.

140. "Annales de Sébastián Brant" (1892), p. 148 and Specklin, *Les Collectanées*, p. 489.

141. "Annales de Sébastián Brant" (1892), p. 239.

142. See Oberlé, *La Vie Quotidienne*.

143. Specklin, *Les Collectanées*, p. 489.

144. Gebwiller, *Die Strassburger Chronik*, p. 74.

145. See Backman, *Religious Dances*, p. 180.

146. Francis Rapp, "Leonard Heischer, Peintre de La Danse Macrabre de Strasbourg (1474)," *Revue D'Alsace*, vol. 100 (1961), pp. 129–36. For debates about the morality of dance see Backman, *Religious Dances*, and Ehrenreich, *Dancing in the Streets*.

147. Gebwiller, *Die Strassburger Chronik*, p. 74; quoted in Midelfort, *Madness*, p. 34.

148. "Annales de Sébastián Brant" (1899), p. 252.

149. See Specklin, *Les Collectanées*, p. 489; "Chronique de Jean Wencker" (1892), p. 148.

150. Rem, *Chronica Newer Geschichten*; Specklin, *Les Collectanées*, p. 489; "Chronique de Jean Wencker" (1892), p. 148.

151. Quoted in Martin's "Geschichte der Tanzkrankheit in Deutschland," p. 115.

152. Quoted in and translated by Midelfort, *Madness*, pp. 35–6.

153. Rem, *Chronica Newer Geschichten*.

154. Quoted in and translated by Midelfort, *Madness*, p. 35.

155. "Annales de Sébastián Brant" (1892), p. 232.

156. See Oberlé, *La Vie Quotidienne*, chapter 5.

157. Quoted in and translated by Midelfort, *Madness*, p. 36. See also Martin's "Geschichte der Tanzkrankheit in Deutschland," p. 221.

158. Quoted in Martin's "Geschichte der Tanzkrankheit in Deutschland," p. 221. See also "Annales de Sébastián Brant" (1892), p. 240.

159. Quoted in and translated by Midelfort, *Madness*, p. 35.

160. Ibid.

161. Quoted in Martin's "Geschichte der Tanzkrankheit in Deutschland," p. 221. See also "Annales de Sébastián Brant" (1892), p. 240.

162. Ibid.

163. Quoted in and translated by Midelfort, *Madness*, p. 36. See also Martin's "Geschichte der Tanzkrankheit in Deutschland," p. 121.

164. See Gross, *Hans Wydyz*, pp. 241–3.

165. "Annales de Sébastián Brant" (1892), p. 240.

166. "Annales de Sébastián Brant" (1892), p. 240.

167. Ibid.

168. "Chronique de Jean Wencker" (1892), p. 148.

169. For Strasbourg's exports see Fuchs, "Les foires"; book 5 of Livet and Rapp, *Histoire de Strasbourg*; and Scott, *Regional Identity*, especially pp. 82–4.

170. See Gross, *Hans Wydyz*, appendix 6f.

171. See Adam, *Sankt Veit*, and Backman, *Religious Dances*, pp. 242–3.

172. Specklin, *Les Collectanées*, p. 489 and "Chronique de Jean Wencker" (1892), p. 148.

173. See Amy B. Greenfield, *A Perfect Red: Empire, Espionage, and the Quest for the Colour of Desire* (Black Swan, 2006). Backman, *Religious Dances*, argues that the color red recurs in accounts of the dancing mania.

174. See Rapp, *L'Eglise et de la Vie Religieuse*, p. 158.

175. Quoted in Adam, *Sankt Veit*, chapter 13.

176. Midelfort, *Madness*, p. 46, also speculated on this possibility.

177. Gross, *Hans Wydyz*, appendix 6f.

178. Ibid.

179. Quoted in Backman, *Religious Dances*, p. 199.

180. See Charles Zika, "Hosts, Processions, and Pilgrimages," *Past and Present*, no. 118 (Feb. 1988): pp. 25–64.

181. See David Lederer, *Madness, Religion, and the State in Early Modern Europe: A Bavarian Beacon* (New York: Cambridge University Press, 2006), pp. 119–29.

182. Specklin, *Les Collectanées*, p. 489.

183. Official letter of the Strasbourg bishop Wilhelm von Honstein (1506–1541) to the clergy of the diocese, quoted in Gross, *Hans Wydyz*, p. 382.

184. See Hanauer, *Etudes Economiques*, p. 40 and p. 94.

185. For the Reformation in Strasbourg see Rapp, *Réformes*; Abray, *People's Reformation*; Brady, *Ruling Class, Regime,*

and Reformation; Brady, *Protestant Politics*; *Chrisman, Strasbourg and the Reform*; Derksen, *Radicals to Survivors*; Leonard, *Nails in the Wall*; Rapp, *Le Diocèse de Strasbourg*; Stafford, *Domesticating the Clergy*; Lee P. Wandel, *Voracious Idols and Violent Hands: Iconoclasm in Reformation Zurich, Strasbourg, and Basel* (Cambridge: Cambridge University Press, 1995); McKee, *Church Mother*; Rodolphe Peter, "Le Maraîcher Clément Ziegler, L'Homme et son Œuvre," *Revue d'Histoire et de Philosophie Religieuses* (1954), pp. 255–82; Eels, *Martin Bucer*; and Klaustermeyer, *Role of Matthew and Catherine Zell*. In 1521 Zell tried to preach from Geiler's old pulpit, but the canons refused to hand over the key. So a team of carpenters fashioned a portable wooden pulpit that was lifted into Notre Dame for him to preach on, which they then disassembled for next time. See Chrisman, *Strasbourg and the Reform*, p. 123.

186. See Peter Blickle, *The Revolution of 1525: The German Peasants' War from a New Perspective*; translated by Thomas A. Brady, Jr., and H.C. Erik Midelfort (Baltimore: Johns Hopkins University Press, 1981). See also Chrisman, *Strasbourg and the Reform*, pp. 149–52.

187. Francis Rapp, "L'Église et les Pauvres à la fin du Moyen Age: l'Exemple de Geiler de Kaiserberg," *Revue D'Histoire de L'Église de France*, vol. 52 (1966), pp. 39–46; Chrisman, *Strasbourg and the Reform*, p. 153.

188. See Peter, "Clément Ziegler," p. 267.

189. For these outbreaks see Backman, *Religious Dances*, pp. 242–3.

190. See Backman, *Religious Dances*, pp. 244–51.

191. Ibid.

192. J. Schenck von Grafenberg, *Observationum medi-carum, rararum, novarum, admirabilium et monstrosarum* (Frankfurt, 1609), p. 136; Midelfort, *Madness*, pp. 38–9; and Backman, *Religious Dances*, pp. 252–3.

193. Quoted in Midelfort, *Madness*, p. 38.

194. Gregor Horstius, *Observationum medicinalium singularium* (Ulm, 1628); Midelfort, *Madness*, pp. 38–9; and Backman, *Religious Dances*, p. 253.

195. See Midelfort, *Madness*, p. 48.

196. For the history of the tarantella see Ernesto de Martino, *The Land of Remorse: A Study of Southern Italian Tarantism*, translated by Dorothy Louise Zinn (London: Free Association Books, 2005) and H. Sigerist, *Civilization and Disease* (Ithaca: New York, 1945).

197. For this trend see Keith Thomas, *Religion and the Decline of Magic: Studies in Popular Beliefs in Sixteenth and Seventeenth Century England* (New York: Oxford University Press, 1997) and Peter Burke, *Popular Culture in Early Modern Europe* (London: Temple Smith, 1978).

198. H.W. Turnbull (ed.), *The Correspondence of Isaac Newton, Volume 2, 1676–1687* (Cambridge: Cambridge University Press, 1960), letter 247.

199. Strasbourg was, however, relatively free from the witch-burnings that took place elsewhere in the empire.

200. Quoted in Backman, *Religious Dances*, pp. 242–3.

201. For changing attitudes toward congenital heart abnormalities see: Katherine Park and Lorraine J. Daston, "Unnatural Conceptions: The Study of Monsters in Sixteenth- and Seventeenth-Century France and England," *Past and Present*, no. 92 (August 1981), pp. 20–54.

202. See Jack D. Zipes, *The Brothers Grimm: From Enchanted Forests to the Modern World* (New York: Routledge, 1988).

203. Andrew Davidson, "Choreomania: An Historical Sketch, with Some Account of an Epidemic Observed in Madagascar," *Edinburgh Medical Journal*, vol. 95 (July 1867 to June 1868), 124–36.

204. See Lesley A. Sharp, *The Possessed and the Dispossessed: Spirits, Identity, and Power in a Madagascar Migrant Town* (Berkeley: University of California Press, 1993) and Lesley A. Sharp, "Social Change, Social Protest: The 'Dancing Mania' in Nineteenth Century Madagascar," unpublished paper presented at the Annual Meetings of the American Anthropological Association (Washington, 1985).

205. See Tart, *Altered States*; David Spiegel, ed. *Dissociation: Culture, Mind, and Body* (Washington, DC: American Psychiatric Press, 1994). For historical aspects see Sander L. Gilman et al., (ed.) *Hysteria beyond Freud* (Berkeley: University of California Press, 1993); Mark S. Micale, *Approaching Hysteria: Disease and Its Interpretations* (Princeton, N.J.: Princeton University Press, 1995); Ian Hacking, *Rewriting the Soul: Multiple Personality and the Sciences of Memory* (Princeton, N.J.: Princeton University

Press, 1995); and Ian Hacking, *Mad Travellers: Reflections on the Reality of Transient Mental Illnesses* (London: Free Association Books, 1998).

206. For summaries of methods of trance-induction, see Tara L. AvRuskin, "Neurophysiology and the Curative Possession Trance: The Chinese Case," *Medical Anthropology Quarterly*, vol. 2, no. 3 (1988), pp. 286–302; Tart, *Altered States*; Gilbert Rouget, *Music and Trance: A Theory of the Relations between Music and Possession* (Chicago: University of Chicago Press, 1985); and Colleen Ward, "Thaipusam in Malaysia: A Psycho-Anthropological Analysis of Ritual Trance, Ceremonial Possession, and Self-Mortification Practices," *Ethos*, vol. 12, no. 4 (1984), pp. 307–344.

207. For an overview see AvRuskin, "Curative Possession Trance," p. 299.

208. See Backman, *Religious Dances*, pp. 215–6.

209. M. Schedlowski and U. Tewes, "Physiological arousal and perception of bodily state during parachute jumping," *Psychophysiology*, vol. 29 (1992), pp. 95–103.

210. See Michel de Certeau, *The Possession at Loudun*; translated by Michael B. Smith (Chicago: University of Chicago Press, 2000) and Aldous Huxley, *The Devils of Loudun* (New York: Carroll & Graf, 1986).

211. See W.H. Phoon, "Outbreaks of Mass Hysteria at Workplaces in Singapore: Some Patterns and Modes of Presentation," in M.J. Colligan, J.W. Pennebaker, and L.R. Murphy, *Mass Psychogenic Illness: A Social Psychological*

Analysis (Hillsdale: Lawrence Erlbaum Associaties, 1982), pp. 21–32. See also Robert E. Bartholomew, *Little Green Men, Meowing Nuns, and Head-Hunting Panics: A Study of Mass Psychogenic Illness and Social Delusion* (Jefferson, N.C.: McFarland, 2001).

212. Erika Bourguignon, *Possession* (Prospect Heights, Ill.: Waveland Press, 1991).

213. Rouget, *Music and Trance*, pp. 46–9.

214. Sharp, *The Possessed and the Dispossessed*, chapter 5.

215. Richard Katz, *Boiling Energy: Community Healing among the Kalahari Kung* (Cambridge, Mass.: Harvard University Press, 1982), chapters 4 and 9.

216. Quoted in I. M. Lewis, *Ecstatic Religion: A Study of Shamanism and Spirit Possession* (London: Routledge, 1989), pp. 18–19.

217. See Rosen, *Madness*, p. 208.

218. Ibid., pp. 214–17 and S. Kidd, *The Great Awakening: The Roots of Evangelical Christianity in Colonial America* (New Haven: Yale University Press, 2007). See also Robert B. Kreiser, *Miracles, Convulsions, and Ecclesiastical Politics in Early Eighteenth-Century Paris* (Princeton: Princeton University Press, 1978).

219. See Robert Mapes Anderson, *Vision of the Disinherited: The Making of American Pentecostalism* (New York: Oxford University Press, 1979).

220. See Bartholomew, *Little Green Men*, chapter 8.

221. See A.M. Rankin and P.J. Philip, "An Epidemic of

Laughing in the Bukoba District of Tanganyika," *Central African Medical Journal*, vol. 9 (1963), pp. 167–70.

222. See chapter 12 of her book *Hystories: Hysterical Epidemics and Modern Culture* (New York, N.Y., 1997).

223. Per Fink, Morten Steen Hansen, and Lene Søndergaard, "Somatoform Disorders Among First-Time Referrals to a Neurology Service," *Psychosomatics*, vol. 46 (2005), pp. 540–48. For recent discussions of the possible neurological nature of conversion disorder see David A. Oakley, "Hypnosis and Conversion Hysteria: A Unifying Model," *Cognitive Neuropsychiatry*, vol. 4, no. 3 (1999), pp. 243–65 and Mauricio Sierra and German E. Berrios, "Towards a Neuropsychiatry of Conversive Hysteria," *Cognitive Neuropsychiatry*, vol. 4, no. 3 (1999), pp. 267–87. For an analysis of the claim that conversion disorder tends to be misdiagnosed see Jon Stone et al., "Systematic Review of Misdiagnosis of Conversion Symptoms and 'Hysteria'," *British Medical Journal*, vol. 331 (October 2005), pp. 989–91.

224. See Mauricio Sierra and German E. Berrios, "Towards a Neuropsychiatry of Conversive Hysteria," *Cognitive Neuropsychiatry*, vol. 4, no. 3 (1999), pp. 267–87. See also Rebecca Seligman and Laurence J. Kirmayer, "Dissociative Experience and Cultural Neuroscience: Narrative, Metaphor and Mechanism," *Culture, Medicine, and Psychiatry*, vol. 32 (2008), pp. 32–64.

225. See Edward Shorter, *From Paralysis to Fatigue: A History*

of Psychosomatic Illness in the Modern Era (New York: Free Press, 1992).

226. Some of Charcot's patients moved in unusual ways due to neurosyphilis or frontal lobe epilepsy.

227. See Shorter, *Paralysis to Fatigue*, p. 175.

228. Quoted in Edward Shorter, *A History of Psychiatry: From the Era of the Asylum to the Age of Prozac* (New York: John Wiley & Sons, 1997), p. 149.

229. See Ben Shephard, *A War of Nerves: Soldiers and Psychiatrists in the Twentieth Century* (Cambridge, Mass.: Harvard University Press, 2001), pp. 76–8.

230. See Shorter, *Paralysis to Fatigue*, especially chapter 1.

231. Shephard, *A War of Nerves*, pp. 57–8.

232. Quoted by Mark S. Micale, "On the 'Disappearance' of Hysteria: A Study in the Clinical Deconstruction of a Diagnosis," *Isis*, vol. 84 (1993), pp. 496–526, quoted on p. 498.

233. See Shorter, *Paralysis to Fatigue*.

234. It seems probable that many, and perhaps most, cases of Chronic Fatigue Syndrome and Gulf War Syndrome in fact have a somatic basis. However, numerous cases of less extreme fatigue are plausibly related to psychological factors.

235. D.N. Nandi, Gauranga Bbanerjee, Sabyasachi Nandi, and Parthasarathi Nandi, "Is Hysteria on the Wane? A Community Survey in West Bengal, India," *British Journal of Psychiatry* (1992), vol. 160, pp. 87–91. See also

David Spiegel, ed., *Dissociation: Culture, Mind, and Body* (Washington, DC: American Psychiatric Press, 1994).

236. See his book *Social Origins of Distress and Disease: Depression, Neurasthemia, and Pain in Modern China* (New Haven: Yale University Press, 1986).

237. Shephard, *A War of Nerves*, pp. 208–9.

238. See Ben Malbon, *Clubbing: Dancing, Ecstasy, and Vitality* (New York: Routledge, 1999).

ABOUT THE AUTHOR

John Waller is an Assistant Professor of the History of Medicine at Michigan State University and an honorary fellow of the University of Melbourne. He is the author of five books, including *Einstein's Luck*, and has written numerous articles on the history of science and medicine.

INDEX